Coping with Cutbacks

The Nonprofit Guide to Success When Times Are Tight

Coping with Cutbacks

The Nonprofit Guide to Success When Times Are Tight

by Emil Angelica and Vincent Hyman

We would like to thank the Edyth Bush Charitable Foundation and the Amherst H. Wilder Foundation for underwriting the research and writing of this book.

Amherst H. Wilder Foundation
Saint Paul, Minnesota

This book was developed by the Services to Organizations' Community Services Group, a program of the Amherst H. Wilder Foundation in Saint Paul, Minnesota. The Community Services Group works in the St. Paul–Minneapolis metropolitan area and nationally to strengthen the capacity of individuals, organizations, and other groups to improve their communities.

The Amherst H. Wilder Foundation is one of the largest and oldest endowed human service and community development organizations in America. For more than ninety years, the Wilder Foundation has been providing health and human services that help children and families grow strong, the elderly age with dignity, and the community grow in its ability to meet its own needs.

We hope you find this book helpful! Should you need additional information about our services, please contact:
Community Services Group, Amherst H. Wilder Foundation,
919 Lafond Avenue, Saint Paul, MN 55104, (612) 642-4022.

For information about other Wilder Foundation publications, please see the order form at the back of this book or contact:
Publishing Center, Amherst H. Wilder Foundation,
919 Lafond Avenue, Saint Paul, MN 55104, 1-800-274-6024.

Illustrated by David Kacmarynski
Designed by Rebecca Andrews
Edited by Vincent Hyman and Judith Peacock

Manufactured in the United States of America

First printing, October 1997

Library of Congress Cataloging-in-Publication Data

Angelica, Emil, date.
　　Coping with cutbacks : the nonprofit guide to success when times are tight / by Emil Angelica and Vincent Hyman.
　　　　p.　　cm.
　　Includes bibliographical references.
　　ISBN 0-940069-09-1 (pbk.)
　　1. Nonprofit organizations--Finance.　I. Hyman, Vincent L.
II. Title.
HG4027.65.A54　1997
658.15'224--dc21　　　　　　　　　　　　　　97-40748
　　　　　　　　　　　　　　　　　　　　　　　　CIP

Acknowledgments

We would like to thank the Edyth Bush Charitable Foundation for underwriting the research and writing of this book.

Many people contributed, directly or indirectly, to the ideas in this book. Thank you to the nonprofit leaders and consultants who gave their time and ideas through surveys, lengthy interviews, and conference participation—all told, several hundred contributors.

Thanks, too, to the following people:

- David Odahowski of the Edyth Bush Charitable Foundation

- Sherry Abbott of the Florida Nonprofit Resource Center for help in research

- Kirsten Lukens and Sharon Kunau of the Wilder Foundation for support in processing and analyzing information

- Becky Andrews for designing the book

- Greg Owen of the Wilder Foundation Research Center for help in survey development

- Sue Dormanen, Kendall Guthrie, and the staff of HandsNet, an online service for nonprofit organizations, for posting an electronic version of our survey and a review draft of our strategies list

- Greg Branstetter, president of NonProfit Partners, University Heights, Ohio, for his generous help in providing a survey mailing list

- Anne Hays Egan, author of *The Devolution Toolkit*, for her work on the impact of welfare reform on nonprofit organizations

A special thanks to the many people who reviewed this book in draft form, including Sue Abderholden, Marcia Keller Avner, Bryan Barry, Art Cross, Anne Hays Egan, Bob Golberg, Bob Held, Sy Holzman, Nancy Latimer, Carol Lukas, David Martin, Patrick McCormack, S. J. Meaders, David Odahowski, Patti Oertel, Clifford Pearlman, Jackie Reis, David Renz, Michael Seltzer, Karen Simmons, Jennifer Vanica, and Kathleen Vellenga.

About the Authors

Emil W. Angelica, M.B.A., is a senior consultant with Amherst H. Wilder Foundation Services to Organizations. He has more than two decades experience in the nonprofit sector. His consultation experience includes planning, evaluation, organizational development, fiscal management, board development, strategic planning, and fund-raising planning. He has also served as the executive director to a nonprofit organization and as director of his own consulting agency. He has published several articles on nonprofit funding issues and has conducted workshops and keynotes on cutback-related topics. Emil earned his M.B.A. in Finance and Management from New York University.

Vincent L. Hyman is editorial director of Amherst H. Wilder Foundation Publishing Center. He has been writing and developing publications on mental health, social services, and nonprofit issues for fifteen years, is author of numerous articles on chemical dependency, and a contributing author to books on nicotine addiction, employee assistance, and rural violence.

"I never can understand how two men can write a book together; to me that's like three people getting together to have a baby."

Evelyn Waugh

Contents

Preface

This is not the book we set out to write.

We wanted to write a simple book that would help people face the kinds of budget cutbacks that we thought were in the wind—cutbacks that we thought would be similar to those faced by nonprofits in the 1980s. Our book would consist of two basic chapters. One chapter would explain what was going on, and a second chapter would list strategies nonprofits could use to cope with the situation. We figured it wouldn't take too long to research some new strategies to add to those we already knew, so we set to work—Emil by conducting in-depth interviews with a variety of nonprofit executives and consultants; and Vince by collecting strategies and background material from the published literature (books, journals, Internet) and from a survey of nonprofits.

American nonprofits, deeply intertwined with the programs and policies of the federal government, are beginning to contend with a fundamental shift in how Americans want to solve long-standing social problems.

We found out that our simple plan wasn't going to work. The change descending upon nonprofits—what some people call *devolution*—is BIG. Much bigger than can be handled (in anything but the short term) by typical cutback approaches. In fact, the changes we saw in the early 1980s were really the first waves in what we believe has become a very large sea change. American nonprofits, deeply intertwined with the programs and policies of the federal government, are beginning to contend with a fundamental shift in how Americans want to solve long-standing social problems. This shift deemphasizes the role of the federal government in changing social conditions. We think it is part of a growing movement toward using more community-centered, locally based approaches to solving problems. At the same time, nonprofits face an increasingly diverse population. Increased diversity means that the one-size-fits-all approach to meeting community needs simply won't work. Compounding the situation is the fact that many nonprofits involved in social services report heavier caseloads consisting of clients with problems more complex than ever before.

So we changed the course of our book. We still provide a lengthy list of strategies that nonprofits can use to cope with cutbacks, and we hope you will view these as one option to the challenges that face your nonprofit. But the heart of our work proposes a different way of thinking about solutions to the problems confronting nonprofit organizations. We describe a process nonprofits can use to rethink their roles and to retool their services to fit with the changing scene—and perhaps to meet mission goals in new and previously unimagined ways. This process is not just for nonprofits with social service missions. *Any* nonprofit providing some sort of social good—whether via direct service, cultural preservation, policy advocacy, environmental protection, or some other mission—will feel the effects of devolution and will need to adjust course.

We have tested this book and approach with many organizations and individuals. Through peer review, conference presentations, feedback groups, and practice sessions, we've only become more convinced that nonprofits are ready to change—and that they are hungry for tools to facilitate that change.

If your nonprofit organization is dealing with decreased funding, increased demand for services, or both, you will find some immediate, short-term solutions in this book, as was our initial goal. If you are feeling just a few of these changes and want to better prepare yourself for more of them, you will also find here a process to facilitate such preparation. If you are in a community with many opportunities for action, you can use the process to link with a variety of people in the community. If you are feeling relatively secure, you can use this book to inform your plans for the future and, we hope, to push your organization to greater community involvement and greater success.

Ready or not, all of us in the nonprofit sector are entering a new era. We hope this book can help your organization adapt and thrive.

Emil Angelica
Vincent Hyman

September 1997

How to Use This Book

This book is not about how to retrench or get "lean and mean" in the face of tightening financial resources. Nonprofits that faced major cutbacks in the 1980s will wince at the recollection of those terms and processes. Today's situation is different, and we advocate a different set of solutions in this book—expanding and deepening your nonprofit's connection to the community; revisiting and, if necessary, revising your mission; and considering other approaches that get at the heart of mission work. At the same time, many of those past strategies can be enormously important in helping you overcome short-term crises, manage change, and use your resources more effectively, even as you adapt to a changed social, political, and fiscal environment.

Here are tips on how to use this book, as well as an explanation of how the various sections fit together.

- Chapter 1 attempts to answer the question What's going on out there? In this chapter, we give an overview of the current situation. We discuss possible impacts and opportunities as a result of the changes under way. We also tell you how a cross section of nonprofit managers we surveyed is planning to respond to the situation. This chapter is background information. Use it to help you understand the changes afoot and how they might affect your organization.

- Chapter 2 presents an alternative model for thinking about your resources and your mission—what we call *arenas of influence*. We describe four basic approaches that fit different types of organizations: *Take Care of Business*, *Bet on the Board*, *Work with Your Allies and Partners*, and *Come to the Table*. These approaches extend from those that give the organization the most control to those that rely most on the involvement of people outside the organization. In this chapter, our goal is to help you see a new way of thinking about the environment you work in and to suggest ways you can work differently as a result.

- Chapter 3 outlines a process your organization can use as it figures out how to respond to cutbacks or shifting resources. We walk you through a six-step process that ultimately results in your selection of the best possible options for your organization. Our goal in this chapter is to translate the information in Chapter 2 into a process that fits your unique situation. This process will work whether you are in an organization that faces an immediate crisis, in an organization that wants to maintain a high degree of central control, or in an organization that wants to reach far out into the community and rely on many partners.

- Chapter 4 is a laundry list of strategies. Use this chapter if you prefer lists as a way of learning. We have collected a number of strategies for coping with restricted resources and organized them into three broad categories: *Financial Strategies, Structural Strategies*, and *Engagement Strategies*. You can read through this list to get a sense of the many approaches possible for coping with a change in your budget and to understand what others in your situation have tried. Some of the strategies apply to crises, others to organizational change, and still others to a new way of working as advocated in Chapter 2.

- Finally, we include Appendices: a strategies checklist, reproducible worksheets, and an explanation of our research process. A bibliography that highlights a few resources we think are especially helpful completes the book.

Devolution—the delegation of power from the federal government to local governments— brings many challenges and opportunities to nonprofit organizations.

CHAPTER 1
What's Going on Out There?

For nonprofit organizations, the question What's going on out there? has probably never been more pressing. What we learn from the media, from our trade publications, at conferences, on the Internet, and from various experts on the left and right is often contradictory, sometimes inflammatory, usually a fragment of the whole, and almost always confusing. But nonprofit leaders must ask the question and seek some answers, or they may get lost in the changes ahead.

Devolution is the buzzword that tries to collect and simplify the various answers to the question What's going on out there? As an answer, it is too simple to suffice for the complex world we live in, but it is a starting place. Devolution refers to the delegation of power from a central source to regional or local administration—in other words, from the federal government to state, county, and local governments.

The debate over where power should be focused and how it should be distributed is as old as this country. Not to belittle the situation, but at a certain size—say, more than one person—all organizations begin to quarrel over the centralization and decentralization of power. In recent history, proposals to consolidate separate funding streams into broad blocks started after World War II. At that time, the rationale was that grant programs could be better administered if narrow categorical restrictions were removed.[1]

> "At each epoch of history the world was in a hopeless state, and at each epoch of history the world muddled through; at each epoch the world was lost, and at each epoch it was saved."
>
> *Jacques Maritain*

---

[1] *For historical information on block grants, see "Rethinking Block Grants: Toward an Improved Intergovernmental Financing for Education and Other Children's Services" by Cheryl D. Hayes and Anna E. Danneggar of the Finance Project of Washington, D.C. The Finance Project conducts policy research and other activities addressing public financing for education and other community supports.*

In the last thirty years, almost every president has offered some new "take" on the historical tension as to where power should reside and how funds should be distributed and administered. Devolution can be thought of as the current resolution of this tension over which level of government can best address the needs of American society. However you think of this phenomenon, it spells change for nonprofits and, more significantly, *for the people they serve.* The way nonprofits work and the places they seek money will change dramatically. For some, there will be less money; while others may find themselves well positioned to take advantage of a new situation.

The current devolutionary wave occurred on a smaller scale when Ronald Reagan came into office. He successfully combined fifty-seven categorical grants into nine block grants with the promise that such grants would bring government closer to the people. The move also cut back the size and cost of federal programs and shifted control over some expenditures to the states. The federal government reduced its spending for programs by 12 percent. The resulting cuts meant $42 billion less for the nonprofit sector over the next eight years, according to a study by Independent Sector, a nonprofit group working to strengthen the nonprofit sector.[2]

In its most recent form, devolution has been expressed through the Welfare Reform Bill of 1996. This bill ended the entitlement programs that provided cash assistance to needy families through Aid to Families with Dependent Children, food stamps, and supplemental security income. States now have the responsibility of deciding how much money to give to whom for how long, within somewhat flexible federal guidelines.

Alan J. Abramson and Lester Salamon have estimated that over the six-year period 1997-2002, federal outlays in the areas of concern to nonprofit organizations will decline by a total of nearly $100 billion.[3] But even if the cuts don't amount to that much, the trend toward devolution will likely continue for a number of reasons. On the political side, it is fueled by many factors: the states' desire for more independence from federal requirements and for greater control over their own budgets; a widespread loss of faith in the federal government; the federal deficit; and many taxpayers' belief that increased taxes will not provide solutions to social problems and community goals.

Social trends also indicate that support for devolution may continue. Calls for a return to community and to "think globally, act locally" signal the end of an era when people thought the federal government could solve massive social problems. An increasingly diverse culture makes a one-size-fits-all

Devolution refers to the delegation of power from the federal government to state, county, and local governments.

---

[2] *Lester Salamon and Alan Abramson in "The Federal Budget and the Nonprofit Sector: Implications of the Contract with America," a chapter in* Capacity for Change? *Edited by Dwight Burlingame.*

[3] *This estimate is based on the Fiscal Year 1998 Congressional Budget Resolution of June 5, 1997, and is drawn from a paper by Abramson and Salamon for Independent Sector, published June 27, 1997, on the Independent Sector Web site.*

approach to social problems less successful. Hence the need to develop approaches to social problems that work on the local level, free of constricting federal mandates.

Technological trends may also be fueling the shift. Communications occur faster than ever before; more data is available, and people are learning that in many cases smaller is better, or at least more flexible. Successful organizations are those that can adapt rapidly to changes and that serve special populations rather than broad masses. The accelerated pace of technological change and innovation favors flexible funding systems that can react quickly to local employment, economic, and population changes.

These trends certainly seem to push for devolution. However, some analysts also note that one political impetus for devolution may be to accomplish major changes and budget cuts in entitlements that seem politically impossible at the federal level. This is because it is easier for Congress to cut block grants than to cut specific programs. By shifting the responsibility for the care of the poor to the state and local levels, the federal government can continue to cut funds with less political fallout.

Our purpose in writing this book is not to engage in a discussion of the politics of devolution. We believe the process has been under way for some time and will continue. The trend toward solving problems through locally based action using local resources is becoming a cultural norm. Just what does this mean for nonprofit organizations?

On the One Hand, Some Tough Challenges . . .

No one is sure what the devolution trend really means. As we write, studies are going on in various states to track the impact of devolution on the nonprofit sector and on state governments. Analysts suggest some of the following outcomes.

"Great necessities call out great virtues."

Abigail Adams

Less money, and less money, and less money

Devolution means cutbacks in available funds to serve the poor, the elderly, and legal immigrants. Cuts are projected for legal services, housing programs, home health care, job training, community development, and other community services. States will have the opportunity to decide whether to maintain these programs using state funds. Some states may continue to fund certain programs; others may not.[4]

---

[4] The Devolution Toolkit *by Anne Hays Egan is a useful tool with information specific to some of the changes brought about by welfare reform. Published by the author, 1997, and available from her at 505-466-0326.*

Increased demand for services

At the same time nonprofits face decreased funding, they will experience an increased demand for services. Fewer people will be receiving government assistance, forcing them to turn to charitable services. Low-income families will experience real losses in cash assistance, heating assistance, job assistance, and other areas. Time limits on government assistance will increase the number of people seeking help from other sources.

Increased competition among providers

Competition for funding will likely increase, both among nonprofits and also between nonprofits and for-profits who previously weren't in the game. Fewer funds will drive up the competition for grants. New funding sources will increase the competition for contracts. And the recent trend toward privatization means nonprofits may compete directly with businesses interested in providing the same services.

Rush to the bottom

Under the new block grant system, individual states decide who to support. Some states may continue or even expand programs that once were entitlements, while others, for political or economic reasons, may drastically reduce them. Some analysts predict that states will compete to offer the weakest benefits, in order to lower the tax burden for their taxpayers, to attract and keep corporations, and to avoid attracting people from other states who are searching for better benefits. Nonprofits in these states will feel increased financial pressure, even as the need for their services grows. Time will tell whether this scenario plays out.

Shifting political winds

One year funding for homelessness is in; the next it is drug abuse prevention. This is not new to nonprofits. However, the shifts are likely to be more localized. Big news in one state is not always big news in the next. The focus will be on what state and local governments identify as a priority, rather than on what the federal government funds.

Heightened vulnerability to economic downturns

With the lifetime caps on federal assistance in the Welfare Reform Bill, states will need to decide how to best help those people who are least able to hold a job. As local economies inevitably cycle through ups and downs, marginally employed people will exhaust their federal assistance. These people will be more vulnerable to economic slumps. Nonprofit organizations that serve these people will be called on to seek creative solutions, perhaps with less funding.

Increased vulnerability to special interests

States and localities have an inconsistent history of advocating for the needs of oppressed or vulnerable groups. In fact, this history is part of the reason why the federal government stepped into state and local politics, centralizing resource distribution. As power devolves back to the local level, vulnerable individuals will be at greater risk. Nonprofits that work with these people will face greater challenges as they advocate for them.

Shift toward managed care

No crystal ball is needed to predict this one: For administrators, managed care offers the benefits of more predictable capitated costs and easier measurements of accountability. Health care will continue to shift to managed care; elder care and mental health care will likely follow, pushed by state and local administrators seeking cost savings and greater predictability. While managed care offers opportunities for more coordinated care, nonprofits that provide these services will feel pressure to align with large health maintenance organizations. These nonprofits may face budget crises as they shift from fee-based services to capped services, and they will face pressures to merge, become for-profit, increase in size, or specialize.

. . . And On the Other Hand, Some Opportunities

The effects of devolution are not all negative. There are many opportunities in the coming change:

More mission, and more mission, and more mission

Nonprofits are in the business of serving people. Times of change are a great opportunity to revisit and examine the mission—to be sure the nonprofit's actions answer the question What good do we do for whom? Leaders in the nonprofit sector can take advantage of the changing environment to help their organizations reassess their missions and focus on serving the community in the best way possible.

Local access to local funds

The incentive for states may be to keep control of the block grant funds while pushing responsibility for implementation down to the local level. Since most funds will be disbursed through local channels, a nonprofit's knowledge of and connections to the local community will help it advocate for local flexibility and needs. It may be much easier for nonprofits to advocate with nearby policy makers than with distant ones.

> "Remarkable opportunities exist for those who . . . have the courage to lead from the front on issues, principles, vision, and mission that become the star to steer by."
>
> *Frances Hesselbein*

Incentive for innovation

Part of the impetus for devolution is the belief that local initiatives will have more ability to respond to and solve local problems when faced with fewer federal restrictions. Whether this will be the case or not remains to be seen, but now may be the opportunity for nonprofits to revisit their programs and seek new ways to accomplish their missions. The nonprofit world has a tradition of innovation and entrepreneurial spirit; now is the time to let those talents flourish.

Privatization of social service administration

Marketplace proponents in the current devolution debate have been advocating that services long run by public institutions could be managed more efficiently by private sector companies. In this argument, entrepreneurial spirit will push companies to find innovative, cost-effective solutions to social problems. The experiment is already in place in school districts that have hired private companies to run their schools. Opponents argue that privatization carries potential risks, including loss of guarantees of fair and equitable treatment and incentives for political corruption. But marketplace ideology and the thrust toward privatization are not likely to disappear. Both for-profits and nonprofits may be called on to provide services previously provided by public agencies. Nonprofits need to be prepared to both compete against and partner with businesses who bring a different set of goals and measurements to solving social problems.

The new environment will reward organizations who not only do well but also tell their stories well to a variety of audiences.

The collaborative advantage

The opportunities for nonprofits to work with each other, with funders, with religious congregations, with their home communities, with government agencies, with educational institutions, and with businesses are already increasing. The era of devolution, with its increasing demands in the face of decreasing financial resources, means that successful nonprofits will find ways to mobilize all the resources available to them at the lowest possible cost. That usually means finding genuine partners and working together on mutual goals—ultimately, a more beneficial approach to meeting community needs.

Reduction of redundancies

As people who have lost a kidney know, not all redundancies are bad. But in an era of belt-tightening, they must be kept to a minimum. Merger upon merger has already occurred in the health care arena. The constraints brought about by devolution will mean that funders will favor those proposals that serve broader missions than the survival of an individual organization. Mergers and realignments of mission to fill unmet needs pose real opportunities for nonprofits who want to respond creatively on behalf of their constituents.

Incentive for evaluation

Nonprofits now have an opportunity to demonstrate that what they do *works*. In fact, nonprofits that lack some system of evaluation and benchmarking may find themselves to be losers in the age of devolution. While evaluation and feedback mechanisms cost money to establish, they can greatly improve service effectiveness. Being able to document success will also improve a nonprofit's ability to seek funds from government, businesses, and philanthropies.[5]

Motivation for public relations

The new environment will reward organizations who not only *do* well but also *tell their stories* well to a variety of audiences. Everyone in the community should know what the nonprofit does and how it benefits the community. Nonprofits that serve a population that has little voice should document what is happening to that population and get the word out to the media.

Building strength through grassroots involvement

Politicians respond to their constituents; even a few complaints can result in major change. The people who live and work in the community and who benefit from the nonprofit's efforts are unspoken allies and advocates. The era of devolution will require involving them in the nonprofit's mission and calling on them for support when legislative or regulatory changes threaten the nonprofit's good work.

How Are Nonprofits Going to React?

The nonprofit sector has grown largely as a result of its partnership with the federal government. Nonprofits receive 15 to 20 percent of their funding directly from federal grants. In addition, 20 to 40 percent of their income is through indirect fees generated by federal programs.[6] In the first round of devolutionary cutbacks of the 1980s, nonprofits reacted by following the lean-and-mean philosophy of businesses of the day. Many nonprofits professionalized their management, adapted and adopted business-based strategic and marketing planning techniques, and set up fund-raising departments. Management support organizations, fund-raising consultants, and specialists in governance stepped in to help nonprofits respond to the challenges of the 1980s.

While the choice of the 1980s — becoming more businesslike or commercial — is certainly still an important strategy for a cash-strapped nonprofit, it is only one of many strategies to explore in this new environment.

---

[5] *For a useful book on how nonprofits can conduct evaluation, see* Measuring Program Outcomes: A Practical Approach *by Harry Hatry, Therese van Houten, Margaret C. Platz, and Martha Taylor Greenway, available from United Way of America, Alexandria, Virginia.*

[6] *McCormack, Patrick J. "Nonprofits at the Brink: Lean Budgets, Growing Needs, and the Fate of Nonprofits." (Date unknown). http://www.mncn.org/newfed/brink.htm#cuts.*

Those cuts and challenges will seem small in comparison with changes in the coming decade. Some people use the term *sea change* to describe what is now changing. While the choice of the 1980s—becoming more business-like or commercial—is certainly still an important strategy for a cash-strapped nonprofit, it is only one of many strategies to explore in this new environment.

How will nonprofits react? When we were researching this book, we conducted a survey of nonprofit organizations serving a wide variety of constituents. We asked if they were anticipating funding cuts and how they would respond to such cuts. We combined their responses with other strategies we had collected and placed them all into categories. Ultimately, we developed a taxonomy of cutback responses, which you can read in Chapter 4.

"We expect cuts at the federal, state, city, and county governmental levels. These cuts will affect the level of program services we can effectively provide."

Sixty-three organizations responded to the survey. The organizations ranged in size from those with an annual budget of less than $100,000 to those with an annual budget of more than $10 million, with most falling between $100,000 and $1 million. Just over half of those we surveyed were involved in human service delivery. Other services included health care, education, and the arts. Even then, before federal legislation officially devolved welfare to the states, nonprofit managers and consultants were expecting major cutbacks. Here are a few of their comments:

- "[Our emergency shelter] is anticipating cuts in federal funding that is administered by the state. These cuts will have a direct impact on the services offered to our guests in their pursuit of regaining independence and self-sufficiency."

- "We will be losing funds from the federal government, approximately a 32 to 35 percent reduction. Our local funding from city grants has also been reduced."

- "As a food bank, we raise money to purchase infrequently donated foods with high-nutrient qualities. There has been a significant decrease in 1995-1996 already."

- "We expect cuts at the federal, state, city, and county governmental levels. These cuts will affect the level of program services we can effectively provide, such as health services, caregiver training, and monitoring of centers."

- "Corporate funding will be tougher to get as other government funding becomes more scarce."

- "With the large cuts in the National Endowment for the Arts, we will probably have difficulty obtaining any grants from them. . . . The [state] Commission on the Arts will have less funding available. We will lose operating funding, funding for touring grants, and special project funding."

- "We are a legal services office. We have had to cut numerous services, including all efforts in education and economic development law. We have had to reduce our efforts in housing, public benefits, and domestic violence."

- "We are anticipating cuts across all financial support agencies. The shrinking dollars will be passed along down the chain, and as a result nonprofit agencies will look toward private citizen contributions and foundations. These groups will begin to feel overwhelmed and will not be giving funding out to many organizations."

In all, 76 percent of the respondents said they anticipated a cut in funding for one or more of their services. Cuts were anticipated across the board, including federal funding (50 percent); state funding (46 percent); local government funding (31 percent); and philanthropic funding (38 percent).

What will nonprofits do about these current and anticipated cutbacks? Managers felt hard-pressed for creative solutions. Of the many strategies planned for coping with cutbacks, the most frequently cited were to implement fund-raising (75 percent); modify staffing and its costs (53 percent); control operating costs (30 percent); and reduce services (19 percent). Very few considered options such as modifying their mission, collaboration, or advocacy. Here's a sample of their plans:

- "We have already implemented staff cuts by cutting out middle-management positions. This will continue if funding is further cut."

- "[We will] raise new funds . . . more aggressively seek out one-time donors to become annual donors; raffle for a football weekend; seek out more grant sources; seek more in-kind supports, such as meals, transportation, and lectures. [We will] increase tuition."

- "[We plan to] collaborate on requests to foundations. The sixteen agencies like ours in the county have formed a committee to investigate foundation grants and we have included a staff person from the county who will represent the government if we need their support."

- "[We will] increase workload. Staff members will see an increase in responsibilities to continue meeting the needs of our guests. Our staff is already as small as it can be, so everyone will need to roll up their sleeves to help out. . . . Board members and staff will need to work together to keep costs down, but raise more money."

- "Staff cutbacks were implemented three years ago. The symphony administration now operates with a minimum staff. This means we rely even more heavily on our volunteers, whom we have actively incorporated."

- "We might stop paying rent for people in public housing or use other criteria to limit the number of people eligible for our services."

- "We are just trying harder to raise funds locally, from businesses, corporations, etc. . . . We are going to seriously seek funding from foundations through grants . . . [We will] add new fund-raising ideas, anything legal that will raise a few dollars."

- "We have hired a director of development to upgrade our fund-raising. We are looking at more efficient ways to buy the shoes, clothing, etc., that we give to low-income youngsters."

- "I will announce my intention to allow short-term unpaid leaves of up to three months to staff who wish to take them during the next fiscal year. I will ask for voluntary layoffs. I will change health care coverage. I will have staff share offices to save jobs and decrease rental space."

- "We will reduce services."

- "We have approached legislators and staff of the governor's office to ask them to review how state funding could become available."

- "Our agency will be starting a for-profit subsidiary, which will serve as a feeder [to our nonprofit]."

We believe that nonprofit leaders are creative, entrepreneurial people.

These responses encouraged us to continue work on this book, because we believe there are more creative ways to respond to the situation. We believe that, given the trends, the typical financial responses to cutbacks simply won't work. Independent Sector has already shown that nonprofits simply can't raise enough money to make up for the coming shortfall. According to its study,[7] in the year 2002, charitable contributions would have to increase by 124 percent from the previous year to replace probable losses in federal funding. During the cutbacks of the 1980s, giving remained flat when adjusted for inflation. There simply won't be enough contributions to keep up with cuts of the size nonprofits now face. Obviously, all those nonprofits who plan to start fund-raising to make up the difference will encounter enormous competition from each other and from those nonprofits who have been at it for a while.

Is laying off staff useful? Interestingly, a recent buzzword among all those corporations that downsized in the 1980s and throughout the first half of the 1990s is *upsizing*. Corporations are beginning to understand that an organization can't operate creatively without a certain comfort zone. Squeezing more hours into the day and more clients onto a caseload rarely produces positive results. Cutting staff may be essential to short-term survival, but it does not bode well for an institution's long-term health— unless the organization is undergoing a real shift in how it plans to do business.

[7] *Virginia A. Hodgkinson, Lester M. Salamon, et al., "The Impact of Federal Budget Proposals upon the Activities of Charitable Organizations and the People They Serve, 1996-2002: The 100 Nonprofit Organizations Study" (Washington, D.C.: Independent Sector, 1996).*

We could paint a picture of staff reductions, service reductions, quality cuts, turf wars, increased competition, programs redesigned around the latest fad or funding source, even a massive shakeout in the nonprofit sector—and, most important, a massive increase in social problems. It's not a pretty picture. We don't think that's how the future will look. We believe that nonprofit leaders are creative, entrepreneurial people who will respond well to the forces and challenges of devolution. In the rest of this book, we propose some strategies that will help.

You may ask, "What's going on out there?" If you get some answers and go back to work with no changes, you've done little. To make the question worthwhile, you've got to ask the follow-up question, "What will serve us best in the coming decades?" In Chapter 2, we propose an answer to that question.

The more people—from all sectors and all walks of life—involved in solving a community problem, the more options for success.

CHAPTER 2
How to Engage the Community

As a leader in the nonprofit sector[8], you're probably first to feel the
squeeze of funding reductions. You may hear rumblings from people in
government, from funders, from better-heeled nonprofit colleagues, or from
the business sector that you need to "tighten your belt" or "get down to basics
and focus on the most important issues or the people most in need."

The trouble is, you know the issues facing your community are not declining. Even as you try to do more with less, community problems seem to be
increasing in complexity. If you never believed in the scarcity model before,
you do now: *there will never be enough money to go around!* You're about to
view everyone as a competitor for funding. Stop this spiral! Take a deep
breath, and look at things from a different perspective.

Sometimes, by nature of the reasons we nonprofit types get involved in
"mission work," we feel solely responsible for solving problems such as
chronic poverty, homelessness, or poor housing; or for promoting public
benefits such as the arts or the parks; or for preserving fragile things such
as history, the environment, or ethnic traditions. It's easy to feel that if we
don't address these issues, no one else will—and the evidence often supports that feeling. Much good work would not be accomplished were it not
for us and our organizations.

But we in the nonprofit sector cannot view ourselves—or allow ourselves to
be viewed—as solely responsible for this work. The challenges facing us—
especially those resulting from devolution—require the involvement and
resources of our entire society. We have more than enough people, skills,
technology, and funding to achieve our visions for the future if we can only
direct and redirect them. We need to develop the will and the ways to do this.

> Fail to honor people,
> they fail to honor you;
> But of a good leader,
> who talks little,
> When his work is done,
> his aim fulfilled,
> They will say,
> "We did this ourselves."
>
> *Lao Tzu*

---

[8] *By* sector, *we mean a functioning unit of our society. Typically, people speak of three sectors—
government, business, and nonprofit. Some describe a* civil sector, *which includes nonprofits,
foundations, religious organizations, and others. Another term we've seen is* informal sector,
which would include community groups, congregations, and less organized entities.

What does this perspective mean for nonprofits facing major cutbacks? It offers new opportunities, provided that you are willing to work differently. But before exploring what this might mean for you, let's take a moment to understand the values that shape and pressure the nonprofit sector.

For some time now, the "business" approach has been hailed as the best approach to solving all problems. Politicians offer so-called bottom-line solutions to social problems; the push for privatization of social services manifests this ideology. The marketplace value system has become a dominant one in American culture. Businesses, like nonprofits, focus on mission and quality of service. But they also hold profit or return on investment as a primary value, and money, a medium of exchange, is the measure of success in this formula. Of course, this value system is too limited to address all of society's needs. Bottom-line solutions frequently don't translate to community issues, because it is impossible to agree on the costs of problems or the cost benefits of solutions. But this is a dominant value system today, and we in the nonprofit world must deal with it.

Recently, individuals in the for-profit world have begun to question some of the values and methods upheld as models. The business sector has widely embraced organizational consultant Margaret Wheatley, who consults with many *Fortune* 500 companies and speaks at well-attended corporate seminars. In her book *Leadership and the New Science*, she writes that people no longer feel connected to their corporation and its mission and therefore do not bring much of themselves to the workplace. People in such organizations spend one third of their lives at activities that seem disconnected from their human communities.

When cultures collide

One result of the difference in business and nonprofit cultures—and the ascendance of marketplace values—is that nonprofits sometimes set aside their values and traditional methods of operation in an attempt to be more businesslike. In practice, this means that when nonprofits approach businesses and corporate foundations for funding, they sometimes develop a working relationship based on the values of (and benefits to) the for-profit organization. Such an exchange involves corporate funding of a nonprofit program that somehow helps the business's bottom line (reduced day-care costs, excellent public relations, or special arts performances).

Without this direct benefit, the engagement may not appeal to the corporation. (In larger businesses, the corporate giving program is sometimes an arm of the marketing department.)

In this scenario, promoting the public good is one of several competing goals. Projects of this sort may be framed as a way to benefit both organizations: funding for one and marketing or special services for the other. However, sometimes the true goal—benefit to the community—is lost sight of by both the nonprofit organization and the business.

Wheatley is not a lone voice in the corporate choir. Writing in *The Atlantic Monthly,* international investor and multimillionaire George Soros states, "Although I have made a fortune in the financial markets, I now fear that the untrammeled intensification of laissez-faire capitalism and the spread of market values into all areas of life is endangering our open and democratic society." Later he writes, "Insofar as there is a dominant belief in our society today, it is a belief in the magic of the marketplace. The doctrine of laissez-faire capitalism holds that the common good is best served by the uninhibited pursuit of self-interest. Unless it is tempered by the recognition of a common interest that ought to take precedence over particular interests, our present system . . . is liable to break down."[9]

If these conflicts between market values and other value systems are being discussed in corporate America, then now is the time for the nonprofit sector to step forth with the contention that no one system can answer all society's questions; therefore society needs each sector's best values at the table to make decisions and move toward a mutually desired future.

Sector Values

Just what are the values of the different sectors we hope to bring to the table? Here is our assessment—admittedly simplistic—of the values of the business, government, and nonprofit sectors.

Each of the sectors contributes to the overall sense of community, but each emphasizes a different aspect of the social contract.

Business Sector

For businesses, the primary value is the creation of a product or the provision of a service that results in profit or return on investment. An important measurement of this value is money. Good business decisions are judged on their profit. The business sector attaches a monetary value to plans and actions and evaluates their success based on their monetary performance over time. Relative to the values of other sectors, business value is easy to measure, and this is one reason it is so appealing.

Government Sector

For government, the value is in serving the public good and, some say, in meeting public needs not met by the marketplace. Measurements of success include conversion of policy ideas into implementation, creation and passage of legislation, service to constituents, job performance, and the well-being of the public as a result of government actions.

[9] *George Soros, "The Capitalist Threat,"* The Atlantic Monthly *279 (February 1997): 45, 48.*

Nonprofit Sector
(religious organizations, foundations, and other nonprofits)

For religious organizations, the value is in the promotion of a fundamental set of beliefs that govern human behavior and social interaction. Measures may include participation in religious services, tithing to support the work of the religious organization, service to the faith community, and membership in the congregation.

For foundations, the value lies in performing according to the charter of the creators of the foundation. Usually this involves funding programs that create the results specified in the foundation's charter, and often it includes preserving or increasing the endowment of the foundation while continuing to provide funds in support of the organization's goals. Performance is judged on whether foundation grants contribute to the positive outcomes desired by the charter.

For nonprofits, the value lies in performing tasks that further the mission of the organization toward some common good or shared concern. (Mission is often defined by answering the question What good do we do for whom?) The measurement may be in numbers, dollars, continued funder or constituent support, or similar criteria.

We have reduced the values of these sectors into a few simple statements—and some may argue that this is unfair. Of course—and this is the point, really—all of these sectors have overlapping values. The place of overlap is in the community itself. To varying degrees, each of the sectors contributes to the overall sense of community, but each emphasizes a different aspect of the social contract. As a whole, the primary *community* values lie in a sense of belonging, cooperation, and the ability to accomplish community tasks. The measurement of the success of a community could perhaps be the degree of commitment and emotional attachment of the individuals in the community to the community itself. This commitment could be expressed in terms of turning resources (skills or money) back into the community; the community's capacity to solve problems and make group decisions; and the community's ability to collaborate and get work done. It could also be expressed in terms of individuals' spoken support of and heartfelt participation in the efforts of the community.[10]

Why have we taken this brief tour of sector values? We believe that the nonprofit sector's greatest asset is its value system as expressed in the question What good do we do for whom? We think that nonprofits need to assert this value. Nonprofits must bring this value to the table as they connect with other sectors of society. Furthermore, nonprofits must engage with the other sectors in ways that also satisfy their values. We believe that the public good will not be adequately served—and community prob-

---

[10] *We base our discussion of community values on the definitions of* community, social capacity, *and* community building *found in* Community Building: What Makes It Work *by Paul Mattessich and Barbara Monsey, 1997, Amherst H. Wilder Foundation.*

lems will not be adequately solved—until these various value systems are brought into balance.

Arenas of Influence

The way to do more with less government money is to involve all sectors—government, congregations, communities, funders, businesses, and non-profits—in solving social problems and negotiating a desired future. Many nonprofits intuitively understand this. They have begun to develop strategies to partner with organizations in the other sectors in addressing the immediate problems posed by devolution as well as the broader issues in their communities. Nonprofits need to work in concert with other sectors to create a common vision and to share the resources necessary to turn that vision into reality.

In short, the nonprofit sector needs a new strategy of *engagement*. By engagement, we mean the active involvement of other individuals, groups, organizations, businesses, and government agencies in seeking solutions and creating a desired future. We in the nonprofit sector need to seek a better blending of the values of all sectors. Nonprofits will have to change the system wherein corporations, foundations, and governments dole out resources—strings attached—to nonprofits who then carry out a program that may or may not be aligned with the values of the donor. For all of us, the focus must be to promote a community good in which each of us has a vested interest. Nonprofits can work with for-profits, government entities, religious groups, foundations, and other members of the community as each asserts its own values.

Nonprofits need to work in concert with other sectors to create a common vision and to share the resources necessary to turn that vision into reality.

One way to think about the process of engagement is to envision a series of concentric circles with your organization at the center. We call the circles *arenas of influence.* Those activities closest to the center are those over which you have the most influence, control, and authority—your staff, choice of services, and so forth. As you move farther out from the center, you draw more players into the picture. Your options expand, but you give up decision-making authority. You have to share that with others, and you have to include their values in the picture. (See Figure 1 below.)

Figure 1. Arenas of influence

Your organization
Your board and its network
Your allies and partners
The broad community (all sectors)

These arenas are not mutually exclusive. It is very possible and desirable to be working in several arenas at the same time. Therefore, by moving outward in this model, you do not lose any of the options available in the closer circles of influence. Each contains a range of possible strategies for your organization. As you expand the number of arenas in which you operate, you expand the range of solutions that can be applied both to internal resource problems and to the work you do to fulfill your mission. In this way, the amount of resources and range of possible strategies expand as the engagement with others outside the organization increases. Conversely, the level of management *control* over decisions and their implementation decreases. The farther out you go the more strategies you'll have. (See Figure 2 at left.) Therefore, the possibility of finding a strategy that fits with your organization's vision and values increases based on the greater range and number of options. Thus, by increasing engagement with others and letting go of some control of decision making, you may actually have a better chance of accomplishing your organization's mission, ensuring that its values are furthered, and preserving that which is worthwhile in your organization's programs and services.

Here is an example from our own experience. Minnesota as a whole, and St. Paul in particular, has for some years been attracting a large influx of Southeast Asian refugees. For several years, three large public benefit organizations—The Saint Paul Foundation, the Wilder Foundation, and Metropolitan State University—worked independently with different parts of the Southeast Asian communities. But not until they joined together in a collaborative project with several Southeast Asian mutual assistance associations were they able to develop a program with multiple benefits far in excess of what any one organization could offer. Working together, these groups:

- raised the money to strengthen the capacity of the mutual assistance associations

- provided nonprofit management education for their leadership and staff

- provided internships for a dozen Southeast Asian community members to work with the Wilder Foundation

- helped those interns earn nonprofit management bachelor's or master's degrees through Metropolitan State University

The three-year project changed the way each of these large institutions worked with this growing refugee community in the metropolitan area. The project, which several leaders from the Southeast Asian communities called the most significant effort to help Southeast Asian refugees in Minnesota, was possible only because the institutions and the mutual assistance associations combined resources. In addition, this approach provided a united effort sanctioned by the leadership of each organization,

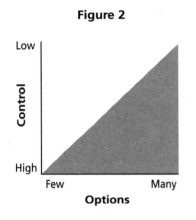

Figure 2

Options increase and control decreases as you seek solutions deep in the community drew significant attention to the issues faced by the refugee community, and marshaled the resources of other foundations and organizations. Throughout, each of the players sacrificed great degrees of control. Yet all were strengthened and rewarded by the final outcome.

For some nonprofits this paradox is simply not believable, and it is extremely hard for them to give up those strategies they understand and control. Some leaders are so concerned with maintaining the integrity and future of their organizations that engagement with others poses a great threat. This is a valid concern. But control-based solutions also threaten the organization. For example, more than one-half of managers that responded to our survey indicated that they have already responded (or plan to respond) to funding cuts by reducing hours or eliminating staff. This solution, of course, is totally under the control of management. But unless it is part of a broader strategy it does not usually help accomplish the mission. It may also conflict with the organization's values and may still threaten the future of the organization.

Creative strategies—ones that move toward the *vision*[11] for the organization and best address barriers and problems—arise when the leadership reaches beyond the organization and links it with others who bring a different tool chest to the project. With different tools, surprising solutions that benefit the community *and* the organization can be constructed.

> "Real control flows from allowing numerous, impassioned champions to vigorously pursue the moment. . . . The odds of success increase to the extent that we let go of the master plans."
>
> *Tom Peters*

This line of thinking suggests that managers and leaders may need to respond to funding cuts in a way that is counter to their tendencies. Rather than digging trenches and looking inward for solutions, they need to reach beyond their organizations and link with others to work on community issues. This approach will often provide them with better options for improving the financial health of their own organizations *as a by-product* of working for a better future for the community. For this approach to be successful on its several fronts, leaders must prepare carefully.

First, they need to be able to articulate their values, mission, and vision for a better community. This enables discussion to take place with others who share in those values and vision. The discussion centers on what is best for the community instead of what is best for and needed by a particular nonprofit. In the case of drastic funding cuts, the nonprofit is not asking other players to save the organization; rather the nonprofit is asking them to work on issues facing their community. If this can best be accomplished by strengthening the nonprofit, great. Even if these discussions do not lead to strategies that address the organization's financial problems, the nonprofit is still better off than before the discussions because it has now gathered the resources to work toward accomplishing its mission and vision.

---

[11] *By* vision, *we mean what the organization is committed to seeing happen in its community.*

Second, nonprofit leaders need to develop the criteria for a successful solution for their organization's financial problems *before* entering into any discussions. This knowledge will enable them to shape collective solutions in a way that benefits both their community and their organization.

As a leader and convener of discussions with other arenas of influence, you are responsible for preparing yourself to represent your nonprofit. By preparing in the ways described above, you accomplish several goals:

- Most importantly, you enter discussions by focusing on the community goals that the organization wants to address as part of its mission and vision. Outcomes drive decision making rather than preservation of the organization. This changes the course of discussion from "how to make sure our organization survives" to the preferred and more engaging "how to solve this community problem given all our tools and resources."

- You bring clearly stated values to the discussion, which become an integral part of any negotiation. In this way you can influence community solutions so that they include your values.

- You understand, from the beginning, the criteria that will lead to a good solution from the perspective of your organization. This means negotiations can occur more quickly because the organizational needs have been delineated and possible strategies structured in a way that addresses both the mission and organizational needs.

Remember, as you move out in the arenas, you are drawing from an increasingly broad range of values. This type of engagement leads to solutions that work on multiple levels. You are solving problems that deal with the bottom line, with your mission, with the desires of the larger community, and with the agendas of all other sectors. If you deal with only one set of values—yours—the approaches you select are more likely one-dimensional. Working with others is the only way you are going to develop multidimensional solutions that address a problem from many perspectives.

In order to operate in this way, you must hold three basic beliefs:

- *Trust the process*: Believe that this course of action will lead to the necessary resources and strategies to address community needs and problems. If your organization is a viable part of these solutions, then you will benefit from the strategies that are developed.

- *You cannot go it alone*: You need to employ strategies that you cannot implement on your own. The challenge is to develop collective strategies; many organizations working together can solve large problems.

- *There are sufficient resources*: The job of the nonprofit leader is to help the community focus on finding the best way to use all its resources to solve the community's problems. This approach changes the course of

The job of the nonprofit leader is to help the community focus on finding the best way to use all its resources to solve the community's problems.

discussion, keeps you from pitting one organization against another in a win or lose scenario, and enables you to find creative solutions that release more resources to address the problem.

From Premise to Practice

What does all this look like in practice? The arenas of influence expand out from the center. Beginning with those closest to the organization, we call them:

- Take Care of Business
- Bet on the Board (and Its Network)
- Work with Your Allies and Partners
- Come to the Table

The following suggestions can help leaders think about strategies in each arena. At the center of the arenas of influence you can

Take Care of Business

This arena is defined by strategies completely within the decision-making control of the executive director and the board. If your organization is responding to a significant reduction in funding for the first time and you feel there are solutions directly under your control, consider this arena for helping you generate those solutions. (Some solutions may require a decision or response from another organization—for example, requesting funds from a foundation or more support from your major donors. However, these actions are not the same as involving these other organizations in a dialogue about a community issue. Such an approach is farther out on the model.)

This arena is defined by strategies completely within the decision-making control of the executive director and the board.

Here are several approaches that might help you generate strategies within this arena:

1. Analyze the budget in relation to your mission, goals, and priorities. Answer the following questions:

   - What do we do well? (strengths)
   - What ought we to do? (values, mission, philosophy)
   - What do we need to do? (expectations of stakeholders)
   - What might we do? (trends, events, and developments)

   Build the budget starting with committed or reliable revenues and then determine which programs are core to the mission and the organization.

2. Examine all programs and decide which are growing, maintaining, maturing, or declining. Manage the organizational changes based on where each program fits in the analysis. Typically, an organization invests in a growing or maintaining program, plans to add value to or divest from a maturing program, and divests from a declining program.

3. Rebuild the budget with an eye toward diversification:
   - Increase the proportion of funding that the organization can raise from its constituents or members.
   - Increase the variety of funding sources in your portfolio.
   - Decrease reliance on federal funding or other major funders when building your next budget.

4. Examine the current revenue picture for opportunities for generating more funds. Look at the entire fund-raising plan and evaluate how shifts into new, untapped sources of funding might generate funds that will preserve your most important programs and services.

5. Evaluate your capabilities and then analyze possible income-generating ventures.[12] Look at your income, both active and passive, and determine if it makes sense to convert some passive sources into starting or expanding a business venture. (For example, one organization converted some reserve funds, along with a small loan, into a thrift store. Twelve years later this store generates several hundred thousand dollars each year; if the same funds had been invested, they would have returned only tens of thousands. At the same time, the thrift store provides valuable training and employment for people whom the nonprofit serves.)

6. Establish a diverse fund-raising strategy. For example, special events can be costly, and headline-sensitive fund drives are fickle. Therefore, work at expanding your donor base by looking toward your natural constituency and its network. Donor contributions tend to be steady regardless of the crisis *du jour*.

7. Put a human face on the community issues that are part of your mission. To influence journalists, policy makers, and others whose help you need, provide personal interest stories illustrating the issues and their impact. Respond strategically to new community issues in line with your mission: You might expand or develop new programs in response to them or explain how the current issue fits into your vision for the future and your projects, programs, and services.

---

[12] *Three resources to help you consider business ventures:* Something Ventured, Something Gained *by Laura Landy, ACA Books, 1989;* The Nonprofit Entrepreneur *edited by Edward Skloot, Foundation Center, 1988; and* Nonprofit Piggy Goes to Market *by Denver Children's Museum, 1984.*

Each example above is largely within the control of an organization and its leadership. Following is the next step out in the circle, which we call

Bet on the Board (and Its Network)

This arena expands slightly from the core of management control and uses the board's network, involvement in the community, and involvement in other organizations. Here, we are not referring to the typical fund-raising activities of board members—asking for money from individual donors or coming along on a visit to a foundation or corporation—but to a much more proactive role. In this approach, the board's job is to open new doors for the nonprofit in areas and with organizations where little or no relationship has existed in the past. The expectation is that the board will be able to form some strong bonds that directly further your organization's mission and vision for the future and increase its access to resources. If you have strong, active board members and they are well networked or connected to other organizations or leaders in the community, you might want to consider this arena for generating strategies. If your board is not skilled in these areas, consider recruiting board members based on their abilities to connect the organization with helpful groups and individuals.

The board's job is to open new doors for the nonprofit in areas and with organizations where little or no relationship has existed in the past.

Here are several bet-on-the-board techniques that may open up new possibilities for your organization:

1. In your planning, make heavy use of the board members who bring a different perspective from the staff and who can link with other individuals and organizations to open up new strategies to the nonprofit. Focus on the external factors that will have an impact on the organization. Once board members understand the needs of the community you serve and take part in the planning that shapes the organization's response to those needs, they can advocate for the organization within their natural networks.

2. Once board members have set direction in the planning process, get them involved in direct fund-raising. When trained and committed to the strategic planning process, the board can be very effective in opening new doors or cementing existing relationships with foundations, United Ways, corporations, and significant individual donors. As board members understand their real potential for community impact, they can take a real leadership role both in the organization and in their communities.

3. Ask board members to draw the attention of other organizations, groups, funders, and businesses to the issues that are important to your organization. An active, well-trained, and broadly networked board can be a natural for considering mergers, spin-offs, and joint efforts because its view reaches beyond the immediate organization.

If merger with another organization makes sense, the board can help figure out how to keep your values, mission, and vision intact while becoming part of a different structure.

4. Ask board members to be accountable to the "owners" of the organization as well as to its funders and the broader community.[13] This accountability to ownership includes ensuring, usually through evaluation and monitoring, that the organization truly benefits the community it serves. Such connection with the mission and outcomes enables the board to be a strong advocate for the organization with the broad community and the organization's key governmental, corporate, and funding supporters.

For organizations with strong boards, betting on the board is a good place to start when seeking to involve more people and sectors. Organizations should also consider using the connections and allies of their staff and volunteers when engaging the broader community. To reach farther out in the arenas of influence, you will need to

Work with Your Allies and Partners

In this arena, you will work as equals to examine the problems and generate solutions that make sense from the perspectives of the community, the partners as a group, and each organization.

This arena expands beyond the organization to include representatives from organizations that have a relationship with your nonprofit. These organizations might include government agencies, funders, other nonprofits that you work with, and businesses from which you purchase services or that serve your constituents. Because you have a history with these organizations, you typically have overlapping interests, common values, similar missions, and shared visions for the future. But a heightened engagement would involve these allies and partners in focusing on both the community issues and organizational issues in a more profound way. In this arena, you will work as equals to examine the problems and generate solutions that make sense from the perspectives of the community, the partners as a group, and each organization. In a very real sense, you are asking these organizations to be part of decision making that directly affects the future of your nonprofit.

Here are several approaches for working with partners and allies:

1. In conjunction with a group of representatives of your allies and partners, conduct a strategic business planning process. Examine all the lines of business for your organization and study your place in the market, your competition, and the fit between your programs, mission, and community needs. Be certain that you understand your areas of competence and that you maintain these

---

[13] *The owners of a nonprofit are those people whom the board represents when making decisions for the organization. In a membership organization, the ownership is clear—members. In other nonprofits, ownership is not so self-evident and the board needs to decide to whom it is responsible. For example, the board of the Rogers Neighborhood Planning Council decided that the organization is owned by all the people who live and work in the Rogers neighborhood.*

strengths while planning. Typically this kind of discussion will result in rethinking one or two programs or services. Sometimes an organization will rewrite its mission or the basic strategies to accomplish that mission; some organizations will even rebuild from the bottom up. Through this process your organization may become more responsive to the people it serves. It may also clarify its niche in relation to competitors and allies in a way that goes far beyond solving the financial issues that started the analysis and planning.

2. Explore joint programs and services with allies and partners. Look for areas where services are being duplicated. Determine if there are joint ventures that make sense and will also help address the funding problems. Perhaps some programs need to be spun off or merged with another organization to reduce costs. Or, it may be mutually beneficial to absorb a program from another agency that is unable to maintain the program; the extra funding and economies of scale may solve your budget problems.

3. Convene a group of long-term funders, explain your situation, and ask their advice. Make sure that your programs are crucial to the community and that the need is recognized by both funders and the community. If the result of this process is renewed support for what you are doing, funders may respond by increasing direct giving, assisting in fund-raising from other sources, or offering less traditional support such as advocating with policy makers. If your financial problems really reflect a much larger problem—declining support for your mission—you will find out in just a few meetings with funders.

4. Sit down with your partners and answer the question What kinds of businesses might we create based on the programs we already operate? These lines of business or expansions of existing lines could be revenue generating and might lead to for-profit subsidiaries or joint ventures with partners and allies. This approach stimulates an entrepreneurial attitude in the organization's culture.

5. Analyze the broader service delivery system. Is the system expanding or retrenching? Are a few large organizations taking over the field, or are there many players? Is the system moving toward managed care, or could it move toward managed care as part of a broader system if there were some leadership? How will things change for your existing programs? Consider convening informal groups to discuss and shape the direction of the broader service delivery system. Explore more formal arrangements that make your organization part of a group that negotiates with policy makers, government, funders, managed care systems, or others.

It is not such a far step from engaging your partners and allies to considering the interests and needs of others affected by the issues you deal with. As we stated earlier, in one way or another the values and interests of all sectors overlap. At the farthest circle of the arenas of influence, it is time for everyone to

Come to the Table

You will need to help other groups understand your goals, and you will need to understand the aspirations of these other groups. All thereby come to the table with the common interest of making their community a better place to live.

In this arena, your organization links with various parts of the community, including those segments with which the organization has little prior experience. Since there has been little, if any, history among these segments, you need to find the common interests that will further connections. This may mean that your nonprofit needs to frame its values, mission, and goals for the future within the context of the entire community. In order to create a compelling community vision, you will first need to clearly understand what you want to achieve. Then you will need to help other groups understand your goals, and you will need to understand the aspirations of these other groups. All thereby come to the table with the common interest of making their community a better place to live.

Here are approaches that may open up possibilities for connecting with the broader community:

1. Convene issues groups around areas of concern and opportunity in the community and your organization. As you convene these groups, decide who should be the formal convener. Who will get the best attendance when calling the meeting? Who can reach the broadest cross section of the community? Who does not have a vested interest in a specific solution but rather is known for being open-minded and inclusive? Consider a nontraditional convener, who may bring new forces to the table. (For example, when focusing on community crime, ask the head of the chamber of commerce to convene a group rather than a more traditional convener such as a crime prevention specialist, block club leader, or police liaison.) Invite the typical groups, but also reach beyond those organizations and individuals who are always involved with the particular issue. This will bring more perspectives, interests, and resources to the table.

2. Organize a tour of successful communities that have implemented strategies to resolve issues similar to the ones you face. Such site visits often help people get beyond the immediate problems to a vision of what is possible. It also shows people the kind of role that they can play in helping achieve a better community. Invite leaders from these successful communities to meetings in your community so more people can hear their stories.

3. Invite funders who share your interest in an issue to fund a research project on the issue. Conduct a research project where leaders from the different sectors are interviewed with regard to the issue. When the interviews are completed, develop a report that frames the issue from the different perspectives, identifies solutions that have been suggested, and helps convene the leaders and the broader community in discussions about the issue. For broadest appeal and acceptance of the results, ensure equal time for each sector.

4. Invite small, mixed groups of individuals to lunch for extended discussions of community issues. All ideas and perspectives need to be viewed as valid at these sessions. Sometimes a guest speaker can be invited to challenge the group or tell a success story. Provide adequate time for people to discuss the issue, develop some trust, and form relationships with each other.

5. Conduct public forums or community meetings to explore issues that are important to the community. These sessions should be open to everyone, low cost, and accessible. They are an opportunity to raise the visibility of the issue, identify people and groups with similar interests, import ideas or models from outside the community, clarify issues, and develop visions for a better future. At the end of each forum, a simple plan should outline the next steps to keep the issue moving.

6. Have a local association of nonprofits hold a conference around an issue and invite people from government, funding, religious, community, and business sectors who have an interest in the issue. Offer breakout sessions, led by representatives of the different sectors, where people work on the problems, barriers, and solutions. This process can lead to working relationships on many other issues.

This final aspect of our model has some implications as you work with the business, religious, government, and philanthropic sectors. Let's look at each.

Businesses

Nonprofits often work with large corporations on projects, as we noted earlier in this chapter. A real risk in these encounters is that the nonprofit backs off from its values and accepts the corporate values. These partners were and are important; large corporations have more resources in terms of money, administrative support, and staff than most other potential partners. Furthermore, it is easier to work with one large corporation than a number of smaller partners. We suggest that as you continue to work with large funders, you be assertive about your own values.

We also think it is critical that nonprofits involve midsize and small businesses. At present, such involvement usually means the contribution of in-kind support: Donated printing, free raffle items, and special event sponsorships are typical examples. We think the involvement needs to be much deeper. Such businesses tend to be locally owned. They are grounded in and connected to the community. They often have a clearly vested interest in the well-being of the community and would welcome being part of the solution. Clearly there are barriers: Smaller businesses may not have the staff to participate in meetings and are sometimes preoccupied with short-term survival. However, creative involvement of these local leaders will generate a new dialogue. Though it may take more work on your part to meet with them, they may also share more of your basic values. Thus, in the long term it may require less effort to negotiate a joint project that better addresses community needs and better fits with your mission.

Religious groups

Religious congregations are also important to community solutions. Many of these institutions are already deeply involved in the community; others have stayed out of the fray for a variety of reasons (the congregation is concerned with spiritual needs rather than community needs; church leaders do not know how to be part of the solution; perhaps no one from the nonprofit sector has found a way to truly involve the membership). But there are many ways to involve congregations. Leaders may let you ask directly for money, seek volunteers, use the building, or set up a partnership with the congregation to address a mutual goal. Some congregations welcome educational forums on what they can do about a community issue. Most faiths include service to the larger community as a basic tenet; tapping religious groups is a matter of getting to know the right people and inviting them to the table.

Government

In the past, nonprofit involvement with government agencies has been in one of two ways: either working under contract as a vendor to or grant recipient of a government agency or being licensed or regulated by a government agency. In either case, government is a decision maker and monitor in relation to the nonprofits, which are viewed as the solution to the problem rather than a partner in addressing issues. This new role may require changes in the way nonprofit and government agency staff relate; however, the greater change needs to be in the expectations that the nonprofit sector has for government agencies. With government having less funding available for contracts and grants, there may be opportunities to look at the other resources that these agencies are responsible for and see if they can be brought to the table. These include facilities, land, regulations, and technical expertise.

This form of engagement views government as a partner and an equal, particularly in decision making. The change is a considerable risk, both to government officials, who are accustomed to certain lines of accountability, and to nonprofits, who must switch roles from service provider to partner. In addition to viewing government staff as representatives of the public interest and trustees of public assets, nonprofits will need to find ways to solve problems inherent in government systems so that more resources will become available to solve community problems.

Philanthropic sector

Many opportunities exist for working with the philanthropic sector in ways deeper than the usual donor-recipient relationship. The grant-making foundation can convene organizations across sectors around issues important to its leadership. In this way foundations can help shape the discourse in a community by identifying the issues to be discussed and by creating forums in which the discussion can occur. Some foundations are able to assist first in marshaling resources from a variety of sources, and then in focusing those resources on specific issues—often using their financial resources and good name to leverage funds from other places. Other foundations will implement programs and projects directly, especially when the projects can't be taken on by any other organization. A funder without a vested interest can pilot a program or conduct a study, with much less at stake than a nonprofit. Finally, the foundation can be a community citizen and come to the community table to work with others to resolve the issues.

Foundations can help shape the discourse in a community by identifying the issues to be discussed and by creating forums in which the discussion can occur.

• • •

In this chapter, we tried to build a case for why nonprofits need to be working across sectors to accomplish their missions. We described the different value systems of the sectors, and we provided a model that shows how the range of options increases as the nonprofit moves farther into the community. Finally, we provided a framework for viewing these options, and examples of the strategies that fit within each arena of influence.

While we believe the greatest number of opportunities will be found as you move outward from the center of the circle, you can also do much within your immediate sphere of control to cope with cutbacks. In the next chapter, we outline a process you can use to generate strategies for coping with problems of finance or capacity, as well as to address opportunities in the community. You can limit this process to your most immediate sphere of influence or broaden it to include as many players as possible.

*These six steps can lead to solutions
impossible to imagine before you began.*

CHAPTER 3
How to Generate Strategies

In Chapter 1, we talked about the challenges and opportunities out there, and we suggested reasons for the state of affairs the nonprofit sector is experiencing. In Chapter 2, we offered a new way of looking at the situation, one that may point the way to a heightened spirit of cooperation among sectors.

This chapter will provide you with six concrete steps for generating strategies to respond to the challenges—financial or otherwise—your organization is encountering. We outline a process similar to what a consultant might use to help you define and understand the problems or opportunities you face, develop a process for generating solutions to those problems, and, finally, generate actual solutions. (See Figure 3 on page 32 for an outline of the six steps.)

This process is generic, so you'll need to tailor it to your organization. To help you through the steps in the process, we provide reproducible worksheets (see Appendix B) as well as a series of questions to shape the steps to fit your organization. We assume that your organization has a clear strategic plan and mission in place *before* you begin this process. If that is not the case, then we suggest you get at least a semblance of a strategic plan in place first.[14]

---

[14] *For more information, see the Wilder Foundation's* Strategic Planning Workbook for Nonprofit Organizations, Revised and Updated *by Bryan Barry. (An order form is provided in the back of this book.) The workbook includes tips on conducting an abbreviated strategic planning process, which may be especially helpful if you are in a hurry.*

Figure 3. Strategy-Generating Process

Step 1: Know Yourself

Purpose: To clarify where your organization is going in the future and the decision-making style you want to use

Responsible: Executive director, board chair, at least one other key leader

Step 2: Clarify the Problem or Opportunity

Purpose: To make sure that you understand the scope, magnitude, and implications of the problems or opportunities facing the community and the organization

Responsible: Staff leadership (usually executive director, board chair, and treasurer or key volunteers)

Step 3: Outline the Process for Developing and Selecting Strategies

Purpose: To identify the people you want to involve in the strategy development and selection process (Steps 4, 5, and 6); and to write a work plan showing how you want to work with these people

Responsible: Executive director, board leadership, and key staff

Step 4: Establish Criteria for Success

Purpose: To develop the criteria that will be used to determine the best strategies for addressing the problems or opportunities facing the organization

Responsible: The board, executive director, key staff, and anyone you identified in Step 3 as a participant in establishing criteria

Step 5: Brainstorm Strategies

Purpose: To generate strategies that can best address the opportunities or problems in light of the criteria specified in Step 4

Responsible: Staff leadership and those who will implement the strategies; everyone you listed in Step 3

Step 6: Select the Viable Strategies

Purpose: To arrive at the best strategies for the organization

Responsible: Executive director, board chair, anyone else identified in Step 3 whom you want to involve in final decision making

What do other leaders do when facing a financial crisis? We interviewed various nonprofit executives and consultants about processes they used to determine the best strategies in response to reductions in funding. The leaders we spoke with had many suggestions for an effective decision-making process. They said the process should:

- Address immediate crises so critical problems can be solved before moving on to long-term, deeper problems.

- Recognize that the ultimate goal is to accomplish the mission (what good you do and for whom you do it). Maintaining the organization and its staff is important, but mission comes first. Therefore the focus should be first on the outcomes for customers or clients, and *then* on the financial situation. In other words, the organization should not just chase dollars; nor should the organization assume that because it exists, it is doing the right work to fulfill its mission.

- Lead to long-term solutions, not just short-term fixes.

- Invite stakeholders to contribute ideas, especially partners and funders, as well as staff and volunteers who will be implementing strategies.

- Lead to realistic and practical solutions.

- Be consistent with the vision and strategic direction outlined in the organization's strategic plan.

- Encourage the organization to look outside itself for solutions to its own and the community's problems.

Maintaining the organization and its staff is important, but mission comes first.

Taking into consideration these diverse perspectives, we have outlined a framework that your organization can modify to establish its own process for determining which strategies will best address funding problems.

Step 1: Know Yourself

Before you begin this process, you need to do some work. We will assume that you are the key leader or one of several key leaders in an organization—perhaps the executive director, the board chair, or a board member.

Purpose: To clarify where your organization is going in the future and the decision-making style you want to use.

Rationale: This step lays the groundwork for all subsequent steps. As you assess your direction for the future and your decision-making style, you will also begin to develop a sense of who to involve, the process you will use to make decisions, and how you want to be viewed in the future.

Responsible: Executive director, board chair, and at least one other key leader.

Begin by reviewing your strategic plan and clarifying your values, mission, core competencies, and vision for the future. (If you do not have a strategic plan, you will need to do a quick assessment so that you have a sense of your organization's future direction.) After reviewing your strategic plan (or completing one, if necessary), answer the following questions:

- What are your organization's philosophy and core values? (What beliefs are central to your organization? What does your organization hold most important?)

- What is your organization's mission? (What is your organization's purpose? What does it intend to accomplish? What is the reason it exists?)

- What are your organization's two to four core competencies? (What are its greatest strengths? What does it do best? How does your organization add value to the community?)

- What is your organization's vision? (What will be different in the world because your organization exists and what role will your organization play in making that difference?)

Now think about your organization's typical decision-making style. Is it:

- a *board-driven* organization, in which a very strong board is involved in any decision viewed as important to vision and mission?

- a *hierarchical* organization, in which the director makes all major decisions?

- a *consensus-based* organization, in which decisions are made only after significant input from all the staff?

These categories are not mutually exclusive, but you should have a fair idea of which style fits your usual mode of operation.

Now ask yourself what decision-making style you *want* your organization to use in the future. Your answer should be either

- *Stay the same*—we're comfortable operating as we have been, OR

- *Change*—we want or need to do some (or many) things differently.

If you answered "Stay the same," please bear with us through the next few paragraphs, which are aimed at those leaders who want to consider a new mode of operation.

Stages of development

Most organizations go through predictable stages of development, accompanied by somewhat predictable challenges. It may be helpful to think about your organization's history and current stage of development as you plan a process for generating cutback strategies. Are you:

- *grassroots or young*, with a founding mother or father? If so, the process you develop needs to recognize the family or community approach that is part of how you make decisions.

- *growing* with an emphasis on putting policies and systems in place? If so, you will need to pay attention to your systems and be especially careful that the decisions you make are models for where and how decisions will be made in the future.

- *mature* and maintaining your present style and size? If so, you will want to involve long-term supporters in solving financial or capacity problems so that there are no big surprises to those who view themselves as your partners. As a mature organization, you are also accountable for your long-standing role in the community. Therefore, the process you use must acknowledge what you have been doing that is of value and should not suggest (or at least acknowledge the potential effects of) any sort of panic or frightening change on your part.

- *declining*? If so, your process may need to call into question everything from your funding base to the programs that you operate to the people that you serve.

If you answered "Change," then you need to think about *how* you want to change. While there are many ways in which a leader or an organization may want to change, following are some of the typical ones we hear:

- "As the founder of this nonprofit, I've always taken the lead; we need to involve the board more."

- "I want to be sure staff are involved early on and can help frame the problems and come up with solutions. But they're not used to being consulted, and they're already scared. I don't know if they can handle the level of responsibility."

- "We've always prided ourselves on being a consensus-driven, egalitarian organization. Given what's ahead, this time I want input from staff, but they must know I'll make the final decisions."

- "The executive committee of the board always runs the show. Given what we face, we need the full involvement of *all* the board."

- "We usually communicate very little with our funders—only what's required legally and politically. But this problem is so significant that I want all our funders involved from the start. They've got to know what we're up against and help us figure out where we need to go."

These are all valid reasons to change. But before you go making big changes, you've got to do a reality check. Following are some questions. Your gut answer of no to any of them should send you on the track—for now—of using the approach you've traditionally used or of making smaller changes. Crisis or near crisis can be a great time for change—but not if it means you fail the organization. Here are the questions:

1. Can you, as the staff leader, make these changes?

2. Can the organization (typically the board members and staff) handle these changes right now?

3. Is there enough time to make these changes and have an impact on the organization's and the community's problems?

4. Are the people most affected by the change capable of making decisions in the time available? (For example, if you have a board that needs extensive training, not to mention an infusion of new blood, it may make sense to recognize the board's decision-making authority but involve board members only to a limited degree in generating the solutions.)

5. Is the additional work worth the potential payoff at this time?

6. Will a change in the decision-making process distract the organization at a time when other issues should take greater precedence?

7. Does the change you are considering fit the potential outcomes? (For example, if you have a hierarchical style and you are considering massive staff layoffs, it does not make sense to consider a consensus-based approach.)

8. Do you have any other gut feeling that says no?

Write brief paragraphs that summarize your position on these three points.

STEP 1 TASK

1. Your organization's mission, vision, values, and competencies.

2. Your organization's past or traditional decision-making style.

3. If a change in your organization's decision-making style is needed, state what you want to change.

This preparatory work will help you better understand your organization. You can refer to it if (or as) things become sticky farther down the line.

Worksheet 1A: Know Your Values, Mission, Competencies, and Vision on page 79 and Worksheet 1B: Know Your Decision-Making Style on page 81 provide convenient forms to record your responses to Step 1.

Step 2: Clarify the Problem or Opportunity

Purpose: To make sure that you understand the scope, magnitude, and implications of the problems or opportunities facing the community and the organization.

Rationale: This step is important because *you must be certain that you are solving the right problem*. Step 2 is where the nuances of the situation need to be clarified; where you determine whether the problems or opportunities your organization faces are short term or ongoing. By the end of this step, everyone involved should agree on the problems or opportunities to be addressed, including the impact on your constituents and services and the amount of any financial implications, stated in quantifiable terms (usually dollars and clients served, service hours, or whatever form you use to enumerate your services).

Responsible: Staff leadership (usually executive director, board chair, and treasurer or key volunteers).

Don't try to solve a problem while you analyze it

Many people jump to problem solving before they know what the problem really is. They often waste time solving the wrong problem or become frustrated because they did not take the time to agree as a group on what problem they were solving.

Consider the example of one organization facing a $50,000 cut in general operating expenses. Before consulting with the board, the executive director immediately set about developing a layoff plan. Word filtered down to line staff and morale plummeted. As it turned out, a board member was able to raise the necessary money in a few quick calls, buying the organization a full

year to develop a long-term plan. The time spent on layoff planning—not to mention the ensuing morale problems and loss of confidence in the executive director—was a total waste. Furthermore, the rush to a solution created the need to rebuild trust among the executive director, the board, and the staff.

Of course, solutions often jump out as you are analyzing the problem. Fine. Write them down, put them in a file, and pull them out when it is time to solve the problem. Throughout Step 2, keep your focus on developing a clear problem statement. Save those great solutions for Step 5.

In our experience, resource problems in the era of devolution are of two types: *capacity* (increased community demand that exceeds the nonprofit's ability to respond) or *financial* (usually funding cuts). Opportunities can grow out of either financial or capacity problems, but may also simply present themselves as new community interests unrelated to any specific problem, such as a vision for a farmer's market. These three situations often overlap. If your organization is facing an opportunity or some capacity-related problem, use Option 1 below. If your organization is facing a revenue shortfall, use Option 2 below to clarify the problem and its impact.

(If the financial problem overlaps with capacity-related problems or some community opportunity, you will need to use both Option 1 and Option 2.)

Option 1: Clarify the capacity problem or opportunity

If your organization's problem seems to be due to an increased demand in services beyond your current capacity, or if an opportunity has recently presented itself, identify the scope of the problem or opportunity. First state the problem as an unmet community need; or state the situation as the community's interest in some opportunity. Then state the connection between the problem or opportunity and your organization. To do this, your leadership team should answer the questions below. Write your answers on Worksheet 2A: Clarify the Community Problem or Opportunity, page 83.

> "The mere formulation of a problem is far more essential than its solution. . . .
> To raise new questions, new possibilities, to regard old problems from a new angle requires creative imagination and sparks real advances in science."
>
> *Albert Einstein*

1. What is the community problem or opportunity? (For example, a 50 percent increase in the homeless population; an opportunity to create a neighborhood arts center.)

2. What is the cause of the problem or opportunity? (For example, elimination of a government program; emergence of a grassroots group with interests in culture and education.)

3. What is the size of this problem or opportunity? (In terms of people, dollars, numbers of cultural programs per capita—whatever measurement seems to fit the problem.)

4. Now combine your answers to questions 1, 2, and 3 into a problem or an opportunity statement.

If your organization's problem is also tied to funding cuts, continue to Option 2 below. Then move on to the Task at the end of Step 2, on page 39.

Option 2: Revenue reductions are affecting the organization's ability to accomplish its mission

To clarify the financial problem, your leadership team should answer the questions below. Write your answers on Worksheet 2B: Clarify the Financial Problem, page 85.

1. What would a conservative budget for your organization look like?

   a. What revenues are definite or very probable? Include revenues when you know the funding has been approved. (Attach a dollar figure.)

   b. Are the funds restricted for specific programs, or are they for general support? (State which programs receive restricted funding.)

   c. What are the implications of any funding cuts for other funders or fee-based income? For example, if a major funder pulls out, sapping 80 percent of a program's budget, will other contributors withdraw their support? (Attach a dollar figure to the reduction; be sure to decrease the revenue assumptions by this amount.)

d. Given these figures, construct a conservative program budget. Include only those funds of which you are certain. Once you have identified revenues, complete the budget by entering expenses. Use the chart in Worksheet 2B to enter revenues and expenses. (WARNING: Assume no new revenue sources. To do so is to set yourself up for failure. You must plan from a conservative budget.)

2. Which programs (services) are in jeopardy?

   a. Which programs cannot be operated unless there is more funding?

   b. Which programs will need to be significantly cut or will require restructuring to continue?

   c. Which programs depend on new sources of funding that are less certain, such as client fees for service, third-party reimbursement, or individual donors?

3. Now state your problem in terms of

   a. The program that will be affected
   b. The dollars that will be lost
   c. The impact on the organization and staff
   d. The impact on clients/customers
   e. The impact on the community

Study your answers to the questions above. Now ask yourself:

1. Given the problem or opportunity statement, is the answer obvious? Can this problem or opportunity be addressed easily and reasonably, or is a process necessary to address it?

STEP 2
TASK

If there is an obvious strategy to address the situation, then by all means implement it now. Don't spend time developing a process that isn't necessary.

2. Are there immediate issues that must be addressed before we move on?

If so, address them or implement a plan to address them as you prepare to move into the strategy-generating process.

Once you have answered the questions above, you can move on to Step 3.

Easy answers

Some problems really do have relatively easy answers. Sometimes money is readily available from one or two board members. Sometimes a beloved program that was already in decline simply needs to be respectfully closed. Sometimes funding is lost because of the poor performance of a single individual or department, and retraining is the answer. Following through on easy answers is preferable to dragging your organization through an unnecessary, time-consuming "process"—especially when the probable outcome is already known.

Step 3: Outline the Process for Developing and Selecting Strategies

Purpose: To identify the people you want to involve in the strategy development and selection process (Steps 4, 5, and 6); and to write a work plan showing how you want to work with these people. As you decide who to involve, you will also be deciding in which *arenas of influence* you want to operate.

Rationale: The solutions you generate are affected by who you involve in developing and selecting strategies, as well as how you involve these people. Your choice of process and participants also sends a strong message to the organization and the community about how decisions will be made in the future and who is important to the community and your organization. In essence, you are deciding in which of the four arenas of influence described in Chapter 2 you wish to operate. Picking the right participants is key, because often these people become your partners in implementing the solutions you choose to follow.

Responsible: Executive director, board leadership, and key staff.

Step 3 is a turning point in the strategy-generating process. It is where you decide how deeply to engage the community. You begin this step having decided in Step 1 how you want to model decision making for the future of the organization; and having decided in Step 2 that, since the problem or opportunity has no ready responses, you will need to develop a process for arriving at some strategies.

There are three interconnected decisions in Step 3. First is in which arena (or arenas) of influence you wish to function. Second is who to select from these arenas to help you develop strategies. Third is how and when to involve these people.

The following list of questions will help you decide on an arena of influence. The questions are keyed to the four arenas: *Take Care of Business, Bet on the Board, Work with Your Allies and Partners,* and *Come to the Table.* Remember, as your organization moves farther out in these arenas, you involve people who are less directly under your influence, and you have less control over the outcomes of the strategy-generating process. Your decision will be influenced by:

- your work in Steps 1 and 2 related to how you want to operate in the future

- your organization's capacity for change

- the skills and connections of your board and its networks

- the individuals and groups you have partnered with in the past
- the degree of control your decision makers require

We believe that, in many cases, opportunities for success increase as you involve more arenas. However, the process of deciding who to involve can be applied whether you want a high degree of control or the involvement of disparate members of the community. You can operate in several arenas at once and you can exercise the degree of control with which you are comfortable.

Following are some questions to help you decide where to operate. As you answer these questions, list the groups and individuals you will contact on Worksheet 3A: Decide Who to Involve, page 87.

Take care of business

1. Which board members, volunteers, and key staff should be involved in making internal decisions about the budget, programming, staffing, fund-raising, and communications?

2. Which board members, volunteers, and key staff best understand the community problem or opportunity and can develop solutions and strategies for the organization?

3. Which board members, volunteers, and key staff will most likely be involved in implementing changes in programming and services?

Bet on the board (and its network)

1. Which board members and volunteers can open new doors to potential funders because of relationships with corporations, foundations, United Ways, and significant donors?

2. Which board members and volunteers have important connections with the primary constituents of the nonprofit or have connections with the customers and clients who might be affected by any changes?

3. Which board members and volunteers have connections with the media or marketing organizations that can help focus attention on issues or help reframe public perception?

4. Which board members and volunteers bring a perspective different from the perspective of the staff and can connect the nonprofit with organizations with whom you may not traditionally work?

Work with your allies and partners

1. Who is providing the same or similar services to your clients or customers and might be affected by the changes you face?

2. Who is involved in joint programming with you and might be affected by any change?

3. Who speaks for your clients or customers? How can your clients or customers be represented in the decision-making process?

4. Which of your funders have a strong interest in your clients or customers?

5. Who makes referrals to you and to whom do you make referrals?

6. In relation to clients or customers, who provides complementary services?

Come to the table

1. Who else in the community works with similar clients and customers but has a different mission from yours?

2. Which nontraditional stakeholders should be involved? Are you willing to consider possible partnership arrangements with other organizations with whom you have a compatible mission?

3. Who might be a candidate for spin-offs, mergers, or major collaborations?

4. Who else in the community might be affected by possible changes in programs and services to your clients or customers?

5. Who else in the community is touched by your organization? Are there vendors and contractors who could be involved in this process?

6. Imagine changes in your organization as a rock dropped in a pond. Who in the water or on the shore will feel the impact? What groups support the clients you support, either formally or informally? Think of groups and individuals who can be involved in your process.

7. Which elected or government officials should be engaged in any discussion of change?

Write a Work Plan

As you decide who to involve and in which arenas to operate, you will also need to decide *how* to involve the people you will contact. Look ahead to Steps 4, 5, and 6 to be sure you understand the strategy-generating process. At the same time, think about how you want to conduct meetings, focus groups, community forums, or whatever other tasks you deem necessary to come up with solutions to your organization's—and the community's—problem.

For some leaders, it's helpful to develop a work plan (Figure 4) to share with board members and others. Following is a sample work plan used by a job placement agency that faced cuts in its funding. (Worksheet 3B: Write a Work Plan, page 91, is a blank version of this work plan, which you can use if helpful.)

Figure 4. Sample Work Plan

Task	Responsible	By When
1. Meet with board and key staff to discuss work plan and assignments.	Board chair Executive director	9/1
2. Ask key funders to participate in a meeting to explore the impact of funding cuts on our clients and discuss our work plan.	Appropriate board members Executive director	9/15
3. Ask chamber of commerce director and several key business leaders in our community to meet individually with board chair and executive director to discuss impact of funding cuts on our community and clients.	Board chair Treasurer Executive director	9/20
4. Ask allies and partners to attend a meeting to discuss funding cuts and the impact on clients. Ask them to partner in a process of exploring ways to meet the needs of clients with reduced funding. Try to get a co-convener for the process.	Executive director Program director	9/20
5. Host meeting with key funders and get their advice and commitment to participate in deciding the best strategies for the community and organization.	Board chair Executive director	9/30
6. Convene meeting with allies and partners and get commitments through a partnership agreement.	Executive director Co-convening partners	10/7
7. Conduct interviews with key business leaders and identify individuals who want to participate in planning meetings and others who may want to be kept informed of progress.	Board chair Board vice chair Treasurer Executive director	10/20
8. Meet with newspaper reporter to explore the possibility of a feature story that clarifies the impact of funding cuts and outlines our process for coming up with strategies to meet the needs.	Board chair Executive director Partners	10/20
9. Conduct a community forum to clarify the issues facing clients as a result of funding cuts. Field questions and generate ideas for possible solutions.	Board chair Executive director Partners	10/31
10. Convene one to two meetings of the partners group to select and flesh out the best strategies for responding to the problems created by cuts in funding.	Partners	11/30
11. Meet with partner boards to get agreement on the strategies to be implemented.	Executive directors of partnering agencies	12/31
12. Implement strategies.		1/1

Do not leave this step until you have identified the people you want to involve in the strategy-generating process and developed a work plan explaining how you will accomplish Steps 4, 5, and 6. Use Worksheet 3A: Decide Who to Involve, page 87 and Worksheet 3B: Write a Work Plan, page 91 (or similar tools) to record your decisions.

STEP 3
TASK

Step 4: Establish Criteria for Success

"There are three things
which if a man does not
know he cannot live
long in the world:
what is too much for him,
what is too little for him, and
what is just right for him."

Swahili proverb

Purpose: To develop the criteria that will be used to determine the best strategies for addressing the problems or opportunities facing the organization. These criteria are based on the values of the organization, the organization's vision for the future, and a good understanding of the problem to be solved or opportunity to be seized.

Rationale: Step 4 sets limits on the solutions that the "strategy generators" will develop to solve the organization's problems. If the leaders are not clear on the criteria they will use when choosing solutions, then any strategy is as good as any other. People generating ideas will waste time with solutions that clearly do not fit with the thinking of the leadership, or they will develop their own criteria. Either path leads to frustration and nonproductive conflict when the decision is finally made.

Responsible: The board, executive director, key staff, and anyone you identified in Step 3 as a participant in establishing criteria.

In general, we suggest that you have *as few criteria as possible, stated as simply as possible*—no more than five. This makes it easier for everyone to understand the priorities; it also frees the strategy generators from having to weigh every idea against multiple rules.

The criteria that you develop should express your organization's deepest values and mission. They must also be grounded in your organization's goals and desired outcomes. They must guide the organization *away* from strategies that focus on survival at the expense of mission or offer pragmatic solutions that compromise the organization's integrity. Finally, they must allow (but differentiate) both short-term fixes, which may solve more immediate problems, and long-term changes, which could include dramatic shifts in how the organization accomplishes its mission. Here are questions to consider as you develop criteria:

1. What specific conditions related to your values, mission, and vision must be part of any solution? For example:

   - *Any solution must maintain our position as the leading advocate for people with developmental disabilities.*
   - *Any solution needs to allow us to continue to expand into Goodhue County.*
   - *We must maintain all services that provide support to battered women and their children.*

2. Are there conditions that must be met regarding customers or clients? For example:

   - *Any solution must keep our homeless shelter open for one hundred clients because we have a commitment to the city.*
   - *Any solution must keep services free to our clients.*

3. Are there financial conditions that need to be solved in any solution (cash flow, diversification, restrictions to funding, timing)? For example:

   - *Any solution must have us operating with a balanced budget within six months.*
   - *Any solution needs to honor the fact that our grant is restricted to providing jobs for homeless people.*

4. What other factors should be part of judging any solutions (staffing, public perception, time frame, special relationships with funders)? For example:

   - *Any solution needs to keep our most visible storefront clinics open.*
   - *Any solution will not affect services that we provide in support of the city's public health department.*

Once the decision makers have developed and adopted the conditions, you are ready for the next step in the process, generating possible strategies for the problems or opportunities.

Develop a list of criteria for successful strategies. Make them brief and simple—no more than five. Get approval from all decision makers. Worksheet 4: Establish Criteria for Success on page 93 provides space for writing your criteria.

Step 5: Brainstorm Strategies

Purpose: To generate strategies that can best address the opportunities or problems in light of the criteria specified in Step 4.

Rationale: Step 5 will lead to options that can stand alone or be combined when addressing problems or opportunities.

Responsible: Staff leadership and those who will implement the strategies; everyone you listed in Step 3.

The length of time required for this step will vary depending on the size, scope, and nature of the opportunities or problems facing the organization. Large organizations may require an idea-gathering process that takes several months and involves hundreds of participants. Smaller groups may be able to convene only the leadership and key staff for a few quick sessions.

Whether you are using large groups or a few individuals, the following approach may help. Prepare for strategy development by writing a concise statement of the problem or opportunity being addressed. (You can simply adapt your work in Step 2: Clarify the Problem or Opportunity.) Focus on the community problem or opportunity first and then on the organization's associated financial problems (if any). Next write a statement of the desired outcome—how things will be different after the problem is resolved or the opportunity is addressed. For example, the problem statement might read: "Twenty-seven families will be without shelter as of June 30 due to changes in our funding in the amount of $_____." The desired outcome might be: "All twenty-seven families will have affordable, quality, long-term housing by winter."

Once you have stated the problem or opportunity and desired outcome, use the strategy-generating group (or groups) to identify strategies that will lead to the desired outcome. Strategies generated by the group will fall into one of two categories. If the group knows an approach to achieve the outcome, then that approach becomes the strategy. If the group does not know an approach that will achieve the outcome, then it may know a *process* that will lead to a solution. In this second case the process is the strategy.

Worksheet 5: Brainstorm Strategies, page 95, provides places to state the problem or opportunity, desired outcome, and strategies. Figure 5: Sample Strategy Development Worksheet shows how the job placement agency mentioned in Step 3 completed Worksheet 5, including problem statement, desired outcome, and four strategies fleshed out by the strategy-generating group.

Figure 5. Sample Strategy Development Worksheet

WORKSHEET 5	**Brainstorm Strategies**

This worksheet will help the strategy-generating group develop options. Question 1 and question 2 should be filled out by the nonprofit leader.

1. Write your problem or opportunity statement here. (This is from Worksheets 2A or 2B. To be completed by the nonprofit leader.)

> Due to cutbacks in funding, we have lost 45% of our Work Opportunities Program budget. This program helps people find jobs. The cuts come at a time when our waiting list is increasing by 10-15% every six months. The result is that 60 people who might have participated in our program will not receive employment training each year; these people will remain unemployed and local businesses will have more unfilled entry level positions. The budget shortfall of about $80,000 represents office space and expenses for two trainers.

2. *Optional:* Write your desired outcome here. (To be completed by the nonprofit leader.)

> Our desired outcome is to train and prepare for employment 100 additional people annually—meeting the needs of the 60 who will not be trained due to the budget cuts, plus the extra waiting list we have developed. These people will be employed within four weeks after leaving the program.

3. Generate strategies that will achieve the desired outcome or address the problem or opportunity as stated. Strategies may be stated as direct solutions or as processes that will lead to as yet undetermined solutions. Brainstorm as many strategies as you can. Then pick the very best ones and flesh out the details, suggesting steps, who might be involved, and helpful resources.

Strategy:	Develop the job seeking portion of the training program in collaboration with another provider and two businesses that have participated in the program using joint staff and space.
Strategy:	Identify an alternative program model that provides services more cost-effectively and uses employers resources differently.
Strategy:	Use volunteers from businesses to serve as mentors to those people who do not need all facets of the current program and can be fast-tracked, saving money.
Strategy:	Charge a fee to businesses for successful placements.

Brainstorming tips

This is not a book on brainstorming, and there are many ways to brainstorm. But here are a few general guidelines that can be adapted to fit most organizations:

1. Keep the groups small (six to twelve people). Brainstorming groups need to be large enough to spur ideas, but not so large as to limit participation.

2. Make the problem or opportunity statement and selection criteria available in writing. If helpful, post them where everyone can see them.

3. Be sure participants understand the problem or opportunity facing the organization and the community. Also be sure the participants understand the process they'll be using to brainstorm ideas. If you are using a group drawn mostly from your organization and its closest allies, only a little explanation may be needed. The broader your reach into the community, the more educating you'll need to do. Prepare a brief presentation for those less informed. Include the organization's history, mission, and values; a description of the major accomplishments; a description of the problem or opportunity you are facing; and a description of the ramifications of the situation.

4. Make the sessions brief and provide refreshments; for example, ninety minutes for informed participants, and two hours for those who need more education about the organization and the problem or opportunity.

5. Provide a facilitator for each session. This person will be responsible for guiding the sessions, explaining the problem or opportunity, clarifying the selection criteria, keeping the session upbeat, respectful, and on track, and conveying both the results and any concerns to the decision makers.

6. Remind people that during brainstorming, no ideas may be criticized. All ideas are simply recorded, without any but enthusiastic comment.

7. Provide some focus, in addition to the problem or opportunity statement, for participants. In particular, groups need to be aware that solutions can include **direct answers** (for example, *combine two programs into one*), **processes** (for example, *convene a series of breakfast meetings with people who share your clients*), and **questions** (for example, *to solve this problem, we need to know more about endowment campaigns; or to solve this problem, we need to research the best practices of other organizations like ours*). Another way to provide focus and to help spur ideas is to use the structure provided in Chapter 4, Cutback Strategies. For example, you could ask the group to come up with purchasing changes, staff modifications, fee changes—basically, format the brainstorming sessions around the headings in that chapter. Alternately, you might assign a specific type of cutback strategy to each group (for example, a staffing group, a fund-raising group, and a productivity group).

8. Divide the actual brainstorming time into two sections. During the first, have the participants generate as many ideas as possible. During the second, have the participants select the two to five best strategies (according to the criteria established in Step 4) and flesh them out so that the decision makers will understand them.

9. After the time is up or the session has wound down, be sure to thank the participants and let them know how you will follow up. At this point, they now feel more connected to your organization and its problem or opportunity and will want to know what decisions you've made, why, and when they will be enacted. You may also wish to leave a contact phone number and encourage people to call you with more ideas.

Design strategy-generating sessions using a process with which you are comfortable or adapting the one described in this step. Identify facilitators and participants, convene the groups, collect the options, and type them up for the decision-making group. Use Worksheet 5: Brainstorm Strategies on page 95 if you find it helpful. Follow up with participants, who now feel a greater sense of connection with your organization.

Step 6: Select the Viable Strategies

Purpose: To arrive at the best strategies for the organization. In this step, decision makers select the best strategies by combining their understanding of the problem or opportunity, their vision for the community and the organization, and the criteria for selection.

Rationale: This step is important because it sets the tone for how the strategies will be implemented. As the leadership decides which of the options is best for the organization and communicates its plan, it also builds on the support and interest of those who helped generate the solutions. It's critical that leaders explain why they selected a particular strategy and discuss the full implications of the changes with all involved. This closes the communication loop throughout the organization and with anyone else the leadership has involved in solving the problem or addressing the opportunity.

Responsible: Executive director, board chair, anyone else identified in Step 3 whom you want to involve in final decision making.

To complete this step, decision makers meet and examine the solutions in light of the following questions.

• Which strategy or combination of strategies best supports the organization's vision?

• Of these, which strategy or combination of strategies meets the criteria that were established and solves the financial problem?

The decision makers then write up an implementation plan to put the strategies to work.

STEP 6 TASK

Decide which strategy or strategies will be implemented. Use Worksheet 6A: Select the Viable Strategies on page 97 as a decision-making tool. After the decision makers have agreed on solutions, begin developing an implementation plan, including how you will inform the people and groups that your strategies will affect. Use Worksheet 6B: Write an Implementation Plan on page 98. This plan should include milestones—measurable objectives with a due date and person or group responsible for the milestone. The executive director should monitor this plan to make certain that the problem is solved as expected. Figure 6 provides an example of an implementation plan for one of the strategies selected by the job placement agency we introduced in Step 3.

Figure 6. Sample Implementation Plan for One Strategy

WORSHEET 6B	Write an Implementation Plan

This worksheet will help you develop an implementation plan for each strategy.

State the strategy, and then list the tasks required to implement that strategy. Identify who is responsible for each task and by when the task should be accomplished.

Strategy/Tasks	Responsible	By When
We will provide the job-seeking portion of the training program in collaboration with another provider and at least two businesses who have participated in our program in the past.		
1. Contact the businesses who have employed the most program graduates this past year to see if they are interested in partnering on this project.	Executive director	1/15
2. Contact other employment trainers and similar agencies to see if they would participate in a collaborative venture.	Executive director	1/22
3. Convene a meeting of the interested businesses and providers to develop the job-seeking portion of the training program.	Program director Planning team	2/17
4. Test the approach outlined in the collaborative job-seeking model with staff and some program graduates.	Planning team	4/5
5. Confirm the new collaborative program model with a letter of agreement addressing the responsibilities and expectations of each organization.	Boards of directors CEOs of business collaborators	5/1
6. Program start-up	Collaborative team	6/15

• • •

This chapter has given you a process for developing strategies to solve your resource problems. We provided a generic structure that you can adapt to your specific situation. You can use the process to involve people very close to the center of your arena of influence, or you can use it to move far out into the community, engaging all sectors and generating solutions impossible to imagine before you began the process.

Not everyone has the time to embark on a strategy-generating process. Some of you need answers, now. We have collected and cataloged close to two hundred strategies for coping with cutbacks. In the next chapter, we outline these strategies and organize them in a way that will help you generate new strategies. You may be able to apply some of the strategies immediately; others can help as you brainstorm strategies using the process we just outlined.

Nonprofits can respond to cutbacks by changing their finances, modifying their structure, engaging their community—or all three.

CHAPTER 4
Cutback and Engagement Strategies

Federal devolution, cutbacks, working smarter, outsourcing—all these code words are symptoms of the changing nature of work. This change affects all sectors of the economy—nonprofit, business, and government. How should you, as a nonprofit leader, cope with this changing situation and the reduction in resources?

We collected a number of strategies from many sources: from a survey and interviews, from books published during the first round of cutbacks in the early 1980s, from a series of workshops held at the Wilder Foundation during that time, and from many magazine and journal articles.[15] These strategies ranged from the specific and concrete ("We have consolidated two staff positions due to attrition and have replaced two others with 'consultants'," wrote one respondent to our survey) to more general responses ("Eliminate all unnecessary expenditures," wrote another respondent). As we analyzed and grouped these specific and general strategies into categories, we learned a lot about how nonprofits cope with budget crises. We also developed a taxonomy of cutback solutions, which is what this chapter is all about.

Predictably, most nonprofit leaders think of two ways to cope with a reduction in funds: cut costs or increase income. For example, three out of four respondents to our survey said they planned to raise more money by implementing or increasing fund-raising activities, and more than half planned to reduce staffing through layoffs or reductions in the number of hours worked.

The methods are based on a "limited-resource" model: There is only so much money to go around, so either the nonprofit finds money to make up for the shortfall or it cuts costs. This traditional approach to dealing with

> "Wringing our hands over a progressively smaller slice of the old pie gets us nowhere."
>
> *Frances Hesselbein*

---

[15] *Our sources are listed in the bibliography. For brevity and to avoid confusion, we did not attribute specific suggestions to specific sources. In many cases, the same suggestion came from multiple sources.*

budget crises may still be your first choice when confronted by an immediate crisis. We call these traditional cost cutting and revenue building approaches *Financial Strategies*, and we subdivide this category into ways to *cut or control costs* (purchasing, payables, facilities and infrastructure, staffing, and service reductions) and ways to *increase revenues* (money management, fees, fund-raising, service additions, and productivity).

But there are at least two other broad categories of response that nonprofit leaders often overlook. We call these *Structural Strategies* and *Engagement Strategies*. These strategies require a manager to look differently at the problem he or she is facing and to look beyond the organization itself. These strategies overlap with the arenas of influence presented in Chapter 2: As the nonprofit moves farther out in the arenas of influence, it is more likely to choose strategies that change the structure of the organization or call for greater engagement of other sectors.

Structural strategies involve changing the mission of the organization, its internal structure, or its culture. For example, the Springfield Fitness Association was faced with intense competition from two recently opened for-profit gymnasiums in the neighborhood. Rather than upgrade its facilities to compete with these organizations, Springfield Fitness chose to offer a range of healthy lifestyle classes. It also improved access to exercise opportunities for underserved populations in the community, primarily seniors, youth, and financially stressed families. This organization changed its structure to continue serving the community.

Engagement strategies require much greater involvement of the larger community—the business, religious, philanthropic, governmental, and other systems in which the nonprofit is embedded. An engagement strategy requires an organization to involve many more people in both planning and implementation. These strategies may take longer to enact, but they tend to strengthen the roots of the organization, as it must reach far into every sector. In the example above, Springfield Fitness Association could have engaged the community by convening its existing members, its network of similar fitness associations, its new competitors, and the public health department (to name a few constituents) to explore its mission and how it should best serve the community given the changing environment. Options on the table might have ranged from dissolution to a sweeping healthy community initiative involving schools, public health, local hospitals, and various businesses—including the new competition.

Very few of the organizations we surveyed used structural or engagement strategies—one of every seven nonprofits tried what we view as a structural solution, and only one of the sixty-five respondents tried a true engagement strategy. This is understandable, given that in times of crisis, we tend to mind our own store first, and we need to act fast. Structural and engagement strategies may take more time than some nonprofits have—although it's important to note that some financial strategies take time to put in place. Engagement strategies offer the organization the *least* direct control over its destiny and usually take a long, concerted effort to accomplish. However, we believe some engagement strategies may ultimately do more to accomplish the organization's mission and preserve its health than the quick-acting financial strategies.

Some nonprofit organizations are already involved in engagement strategies. Larger nonprofits also may work with allies to educate policy makers on the issues, conduct broad-based public relations campaigns, or change the attitude of the local chamber of commerce. All of these efforts push the organization farther into its community and often broaden the geographic boundaries of its community as well. The payoffs can be very large.

The trouble with cutbacks . . .

The following is the report of a work study engineer, a specialist in method engineering, after a visit to a symphony concert at the Royal Festival Hall in London.

How to Be Efficient, with Fewer Violins[16]

For considerable periods, the four oboe players had nothing to do. The number should be reduced and the work spread more evenly over the whole of the concert, thus eliminating peaks of activity.

All the twelve violins were playing identical notes; this seems an unnecessary duplication. The staff of this section should be drastically cut. If a larger volume of sound is required, it could be obtained by electronic apparatus.

Much effort was absorbed in the playing of demi-semi-quavers; this seems to be an unnecessary refinement. It is recommended that all notes should be rounded up to the nearest semi-quaver. If this were done, it would be possible to use trainees and lower-grade operatives more extensively.

There seems to be too much repetition of some musical passages. Scores should be drastically pruned. No useful purpose is served by repeating on the horns a passage which has already been handled by the strings. It is estimated that if all redundant passages were eliminated, the whole concert time of two hours could be reduced to twenty minutes and there would be no need for intermission.

The conductor agrees generally with these recommendations, but expressed the opinion that there might be some falling off in box-office receipts. In that unlikely event, it should be possible to close sections of the auditorium entirely, with a consequential saving of overhead expenses, lighting, attendants, etc. If worse came to worst, the whole thing could be abandoned and the public could go to the Albert Hall instead.

—Anonymous memorandum circulating in London, 1955

---

[16] *We have made considerable effort to track down a published source for this little memo. In the midst of a move, Vince found it on an old, faded sheet of paper, hand-typed, and inserted in an old book; it dropped out just in time for insertion here. If you are the author or publisher, or know of the author, thank you, and please contact us so we can give you due credit and formally request permission to use this wonderful memo.*

How to Use the Strategies List

We offer the list that follows as a thinking tool and as a route to direct action. It should help you think creatively about your organization, its culture, its mission, its response to immediate financial crises, and its long-term preparation for the future. (An abbreviated version of the list appears in Appendix A.)

You may want to use some of the strategies immediately or simply build them into your day-to-day operations. By studying the list, you may be able to avoid reducing services for your community, cutting staff in ways that demoralize and contradict personal or organizational values, or trying to extract more funds from the same overburdened sources. You may find yourself involved in new activities that push you farther into the community, embarking on a process that involves you with local small businesses, civic groups, religious organizations, and others in a new spirit of collaboration.

The list is by no means complete, nor is it the only way to organize strategies. As you read it, you'll see some strategies that seem to be force-fit into certain categories, and some that overlap or could fit in more than one category. The categories may create a barrier, especially as you find creative ways to link the various strategies. The point is, use these suggestions as a starting point for your own brainstorming, and use the categories to help you organize your thoughts and analyze your current approach to fulfilling your mission. But don't get locked into any one strategy—cut them up, pull them out of a hat, mix and match them. Do whatever helps you spark new ideas that fit your specific situation.

No doubt you'll think of many more strategies than we've listed here, as well as other ways to organize them. Tell us about them, and we'll include them in the next edition of this book.[17]

> "Let's not sigh and ask ourselves about the state of the arts anymore. . . . Better to say . . . 'I can see there are many who need inspiration and fresh perspectives. Isn't it lucky that as an artist I have such an important role to play in my time?'"
>
> *Joe Goode*

---

[17] *We have placed all these strategies on the Wilder Foundation's Web site at www.wilder.org. You can send strategies to us electronically by visiting that site; quarterly, we will edit and enter them on the list. Or, you can send them to us via the postal service: Wilder Publishing Center, Cutback Strategies, 919 Lafond Avenue, St. Paul, MN 55104. Be sure to include your name, address, phone number, and a note giving us permission to list the strategy in our next edition.*

The Strategies

Please note: **Just because we've listed a strategy, don't assume we endorse it. We have tried to list every strategy we could find regardless of our own opinions of them. Some strategies may conflict with your mission, values, or human resource policies. Some may jeopardize your nonprofit status or create taxable unrelated business income. Some may require legal or other advice. Some may conflict with the terms and conditions of your existing grants and contracts. Some short-term strategies may have long-term costs. You'll have to check out all of those possibilities as you explore options for change.**

I. Financial Strategies

A. Strategies to cut or control costs

General advice

1. Make cost cutting a daily activity (but don't lose sight of quality in the process).

2. Hold organization-wide meetings on cost savings.

3. Use bottom-up budgeting. In this system, the top administrator—after training the staff—delegates responsibility and authority for budget items to line managers, who are closer to service provision. If a program actually beats its budget, that program keeps half of the difference to use as it sees fit.

4. Have a tight set of financial controls in place so you are free to attend to mission-related matters without having to watch your back.

5. Use a finance/mission matrix to guide program decisions. Apply the following grid to each program or service offered by your nonprofit:

	Low fit with mission	High fit with mission
Low $ support required	*consider cuts*	*keep program as is*
High $ support required	*cut here*	*find better financing strategy*

Analyze purchasing

1. Improve purchasing procedures to cut wasteful expenditures.

2. Reduce the cost of supplies.

3. Seek in-kind contributions of supplies, printing, and so forth.

4. Tap into your stakeholders and constituents as potential contributors of material resources.

5. Network with others to get better prices on supplies through group purchasing. (In some states, statewide nonprofit associations have done this.)

6. Negotiate for better prices or terms from your long-term, reliable suppliers; if necessary, seek new bids from new suppliers—but don't underestimate the value of goodwill and long-standing relationships.

7. Analyze ongoing purchases to see if they are truly necessary. For example, use only one letterhead for the entire organization rather than separate letterheads for separate programs.

8. Simplify paperwork and reduce the use of forms.

9. Use electronic files in place of multiple paper copies to save paper, storage, and support staff costs.

10. Barter with other nonprofits. Barter with everyone.

11. Refurbish and reuse supplies you might normally dispose. For example, if your organization uses many computer printouts, purchase a ribbon re-inker and save the cost of new ribbons; turn scrap printouts into writing pads; turn shredded printouts into packing material.

Adjust payables

1. Consolidate debt or restructure to reduce monthly payments.

2. Capitalize on the goodwill you've built up with creditors and others, and let them know in advance you'll have problems making payments. Develop plans *before* the crunch.

3. Make small, partial payments; delay paying suppliers by negotiating schedules without increasing the total cost or damaging your credit reputation.

4. Barter with another organization for needed services. For example, exchange your bookkeeping skills for another organization's grant-writing skills.

Evaluate facilities and infrastructure

1. Share space with another organization.

2. Temporarily delay maintenance. (Note that this strategy can result in higher costs in the long run.)

3. Share costs of selected maintenance activities with other organizations (snowplowing, night cleanup).

4. Reduce or increase building temperature, within a range that does not harm productivity by making staff uncomfortable.

5. Move to a cheaper space or reduce the size of the space you are using.

6. Negotiate a decreased rent with your landlord, who may prefer a good tenant at a slightly reduced rate than no tenant at all.

7. Convert to split work shifts to save space.

8. Encourage employees to office at home; purchase home office equipment if needed. Some employees may see this as a benefit.

9. Find a cheaper phone system; eliminate toll-free lines.

10. Eliminate, condense, or consolidate newsletters and program brochures. (Has your in-house public relations department become a brochure machine?)

11. Eliminate organizational vehicles; use less costly and more energy-efficient vehicles.

12. Save energy; reduce the cost of lighting, heating, cooling, water, sewage, and waste removal.

Modify staffing and related costs

1. Reduce hours.

2. Reduce workweek.

3. Lay off staff.

4. Freeze hiring.

5. Pay staff at 90 percent of their current rate; pay the remaining 10 percent at the end of each quarter based on the financial situation of the organization.

6. Share jobs or consolidate staff.

7. Increase workload.

8. Use volunteers and graduate interns; make fringe benefits available to volunteers to attract them.

9. Hire only when a job appears to have a long life-expectancy; contract out for shorter-term projects.

10. Terminate poor performers.

11. Create meaningful professional development tracks that do not funnel high performers into management simply for better compensation.

12. Hire temporary staff or consultants.

13. Use external services for functions previously performed internally ("outsource").

14. Cut or freeze wages.

15. Offer (or institute) unpaid leaves of absence.

16. Flatten the organization; remove management layers; eliminate highly paid administrators.

17. Reduce or restructure vacation, sick leave, health, education, and other benefits and perks; increase medical co-pay.

18. Reduce or cease all staff training and development activities.

19. Limit or eliminate travel.

20. Cancel subscriptions and publications purchases; use the Internet or local or university libraries.

21. Cancel professional association memberships.

22. Switch to a direct reimbursement status for unemployment compensation.

23. Ask your board not to submit expenses for reimbursement.

24. Offer voluntary staff cost-reduction packages, including early retirement, voluntary layoffs, and moving to part-time or consultant status.

25. Explore the possibility of keeping some staff as volunteers rather than as paid employees. This approach has worked with staff who became employed after volunteering and with those who are nearing a life transition.

26. Share staff with other organizations in order to reduce your total costs while retaining needed skills.

Reduce services

1. Analyze the alignment of your programs and services with your mission and financial goals; rate each program or service according to its harmony with the mission and its contribution to financial security. (For one approach to this, see the grid under Strategies to cut or control costs/general advice/#5.)

2. Reduce or eliminate noncore programs or services.

3. Limit eligibility for programs to the most needy.

4. Limit eligibility for programs to those people most able to pay.

5. Reduce the number of clients served.

6. Reduce or eliminate core programs or services.

7. Temporarily shut down some or all services.

8. Plan to go out of business as humanely as possible.

B. Strategies to increase revenues

General advice

1. Teach managers and supervisors to run brainstorming sessions, and then involve the entire organization in finding creative ways to increase income.

2. Evaluate ideas for new income in terms of these criteria: speed, cost-effectiveness, likelihood of success, burden on internal resources, potential side effects.

3. Analyze the effects of increased or altered fee structures across the entire organization to see how alterations in one area will affect the financial structure of another area. This is especially important in larger organizations, where clients may encounter vastly different fees for similar services, creating a public relations nightmare.

4. Develop a long-term fund-raising plan and supporting strategies.

5. Don't chase dollars—that is, don't change your programs, services, products, or mission simply to protect or enhance your funding stream. Seek strategic changes that fit with your organization's vision and strengths and that result in increased funding.

Manage money differently

1. Speed the inflow of cash by invoicing promptly, rewarding early payers with discounts, punishing late payers with fees, and keeping up with overdue fees.

2. Talk with funders to see if you can get grants in the door earlier than the promised date.

3. Change management of cash reserves to improve unearned income; find a financial planning group that specializes in the conditions of nonprofits your size.

4. Sell assets.

5. Spend down reserves.

6. Borrow money.

7. Analyze your revenue base; diversify your sources of income to improve the mix of resources.

Increase fees

1. Analyze all the costs for providing a service to be sure you understand what the service costs and how it fits with your financial situation.

2. Increase fees.

3. Change your fee structure to result in increased income; itemize service components that were previously rolled into one fee. For example, charge for workbooks and materials that were previously included in tuition.

Initiate or accelerate fund-raising[18]

1. Research your larger community and current donors to uncover the factors that influence or restrict giving; develop strategies based on that research.

2. Hire a development director or staff, or use an external fund-raising consultant.

3. Add special events/fund drives.

4. Institute charitable gambling.

5. Increase board involvement in fund-raising.

6. Increase planned giving.

7. Build an endowment.

8. Increase activity of current donors; seek major gifts.

9. Find new donors and diversify your funding base.

10. When fund-raising, reach out to under-asked populations, particularly minorities and young people. (According to a 1996 study by Independent Sector, when minorities are asked to donate, 78 percent do, yet such groups are not approached often enough.)

11. Collaborate on fund drives; join a federated fund drive.

12. Involve constituents, funders, and other stakeholders in the search for new resources.

13. Link with a business to receive a percentage of sales on a particular day; link with a credit card company to receive a percentage of charges.

14. Seek in-kind contributions that can be converted to cash. For example, accept a large donation of outdated computers even though you don't need all of them, and then sell them to a computer salvage or asset recovery company.

15. Increase the search for foundation and government grants.

Expand or add services

1. Conduct focus groups among constituents to determine which services to expand or which new services are needed.

2. Boost enrollment in or expand offerings of successful services.

3. Sell staff expertise and time to other organizations. For example, sell clerical, accounting, or grant-writing skills.

4. Add an income-generating product or service.

---

[18] *Michael Seltzer, in* Securing Your Organization's Future *(Foundation Center, 1987), presents a helpful taxonomy of revenue and fund-raising sources. He divides these sources into individual donors; foundations; businesses and corporations; federated fund-raising associations; local, state, and federal government; community, city, and national associations and service clubs; and local, regional, and national religious bodies.*

5. Rent office space or equipment to others; rent little-used office equipment to others, or rent it out during down time.

6. Don't give away valuable information that others need unless it is part of your mission. For example, rent your mailing list to other organizations or list brokers; sell information that you collect as part of a research project.

7. Develop products based on your organization's expertise and sell them. For example, a violence prevention program packaged and sold its school-based prevention program in a video and workbook form.

8. Develop products related to your organization's mission and sell them. For example, sell slogan T-shirts made by at-risk youth in an after-school program.

9. Start a business that serves your constituents. For example, open a grocery store in the neighborhood where you offer employment counseling.

10. Start a business that trains your clients and fulfills your mission. For example, a youth center in San Francisco opened an ice cream parlor staffed by its clients, including formerly homeless and run-away youths.

11. Seek related niche markets to expand into. For example, expand in-house training services to reach a new audience, such as adults reentering the workforce.

12. Charge others for a service you must have. For example, if the grounds crew operates a snowplow during the winter, sell the service to other organizations or homes in the community.

13. Develop a catalog of products used by your organization and other nonprofits. Sell these products, collecting a margin on each.

14. Serve as the fiscal agent for other compatible organizations, charging a fee for your services. (Be sure to investigate liability issues connected with this strategy.)

Increase productivity

1. Provide incentives for productive staff or teams.

2. Change the mix of income-producing, support, and management staff to favor the most productive areas.

3. Focus on quality improvements in effectiveness, such as eliminating errors, unnecessary meetings, and redundant processes and services. Find ways to simplify production or service delivery without loss of quality.

4. Invest in a strong, well-educated staff who advocate for the mission and help manage from the bottom up. Provide training as needed.

5. Research and implement current "best practice" in all functions, from management to support to service delivery.

6. Upgrade staff as you cut back, using a strategic, analytic approach to decide what functions you keep and what functions you change.

7. Invest in technology that improves productivity or enables you to reduce staff.

II. Structural Strategies

General advice

1. Find out what's right and what's wrong. Thoroughly analyze the situation and the forces affecting your organization. The analysis should include finances, client satisfaction, program outcomes, and competition or redundancy with other services in the community.

2. When making a restructuring move that involves innovation and major change, follow the "51 Percent Rule." In practice, this means more than half the people in an organization must be at least familiar with a new idea and in favor of exploring it. To get to this point, use a systematic but informal approach of one-on-one, small group, and executive team discussions.

3. Use every communications network available to explore ways to change your mission or work style, including professional, academic, foundation, business, and online networks.

4. Understand your organization's capabilities and how it adds value to the community. Work from those strengths.

Modify the mission

1. Reexamine your mission and prepare to redesign your organization based on that examination. Be sure that your mission is still viable and needed in the current situation.

2. Change your mission to be sure you are building your clients' capacity to solve their own problems rather than simply providing service.

3. Explore your vision of what the community needs and how your organization fits within the community. Realign the mission to fit with that vision.

4. Change your mission to enable your organization to respond to rapidly changing conditions, and train your staff to make changes that keep the focus on the mission rather than on the survival of individual programs.

5. Move out of direct support services and take on prevention services; move "upstream" on the service chain to prevent problems before they occur.

6. Adjust your mission so you can become a pilot site for some foundation, academic, or government program.

Modify the organization's structure

1. Increase your understanding of the external environment. Analyze what other organizations are doing and eliminate redundant practices or combine them to improve services.

2. Position yourself higher in the "food chain" when intense competition accompanies a changing environment. For example, a provider of elderly services negotiated major contracts with health maintenance organizations in anticipation of legislation that would affect reimbursement for elder care.

3. Respond to a changing environment by changing your programs. For example, a decade ago small liberal arts colleges began offering more business and applied science courses as younger students perceived less value in a traditional liberal arts baccalaureate. Shortly thereafter, universities began offering masters of arts in liberal studies as older students, seeking relief from the pressures of specialization, sought the enrichment of a liberal arts education.

4. Spin off a struggling or "orphan" program, its resources, and its staff to another organization where it has a better chance to thrive.

5. Acquire a competitor's or an ally's program if it complements your current mission, thereby achieving economies of scale. (Enter such acquisitions carefully; ask why the organization wants to be acquired.)

6. Relocate with a group of other organizations whose services, corporate culture, and clientele complement yours to create a "one-stop shop" and improve accessibility for clients. (This approach may also reduce the costs of outreach and enable shared infrastructure.)

7. Become a for-profit. For example, the board of directors of a failing chemical dependency training and publishing organization sold the organization to an entrepreneur who specialized in turnarounds. The organization regained solvency and continues to accomplish its mission.

8. Add a for-profit subsidiary. For example, start a direct mail company that sells products your constituents are likely to buy. In cases where special financing and tax assistance are available to attract businesses, it may actually be cheaper to set up shop as a for-profit than as a nonprofit.

9. Be acquired by a for-profit.

Modify the organization's culture

1. Build relationships with potential funders without seeking funds. Enlist their support in modifying the organization's mission, structure, or programs, and then ask for funds to support those changes.

2. Share resources and expenses with other organizations that have similar needs.

3. Make your services more culturally sensitive. You can't afford to turn away any client, any volunteer, any donor, or any potential staff person simply because you don't take the time to get to know that person.

4. Educate the board of directors to make them more effective; help them think in terms of both the mission and the financial bottom line. Add business-oriented board members.

5. Mobilize everyone in the organization to help market its mission, message, services, and needs.[19]

6. Tear down bureaucracies that interfere with the creative flow of ideas.

7. Replicate rather than reinvent. When it is time to add a new service or program, uncover the best examples you can and seek to replicate them; avoid the tendency to assume your organization is better off designing a program from the ground up.

8. Link with a complementary but different organization to bring resources into your organization. For example, in Milford, Connecticut, people who commit minor offenses have the option of making donations to charity rather than face trial and fines. The program benefits minor offenders, who avoid a record; local nonprofits, which gain needed donations; and the court system, which avoids getting bogged down adjudicating minor offenses.

9. Take a more entrepreneurial approach to accomplishing your mission.

III. Engagement Strategies

General advice

1. See your organization as embedded in the community. Seek widespread participation from all sectors: community residents, government, businesses, civic groups, religious groups, educational institutions, other nonprofits, and foundations.

2. Assert your mission and your values as you collaborate.

---

[19] Marketing Workbook for Nonprofit Organizations Volume II: Mobilize People for Marketing Success *by Minneapolis nonprofit marketing consultant Gary Stern describes in detail how to turn out every constituent to accomplish a marketing goal, and it includes many fine examples of organizations who use this approach. (See order form at the back of this book.)*

3. Be clear about your capabilities, strengths, and how you make the community a better place. Focus on these attributes as you seek to engage others.

4. Rely on individual relationships to engage other sectors.

5. Be patient but persistent.

Engage other nonprofits

1. Be part of state and national nonprofit associations, and help them educate policy makers, funders, community leaders, and business leaders about the work of nonprofits.

2. Form associations to negotiate with contracting agencies as a block, thereby improving client advocacy, service fees, and working conditions.

3. Establish cooperative programs with other nonprofits. This will increase the number of stakeholders in your organization and in the other nonprofits as well.

4. Collaborate with like-minded nonprofits to provide service, create and implement marketing plans, and share products, costs, and resources.[20]

5. Seek funding to support collaborative efforts.

6. Develop a bartering resource system with other nonprofits to create additional resources without increasing expenses.

7. Create a nonprofit insurance company to insure nonprofits; return surplus income to policyholders.

8. Pool funds with other nonprofits to get a better return on the investment of capital. (This can be a risky strategy.)

9. Merge with another nonprofit or other nonprofits. Combine with other organizations whose services complement yours. Form a "vertically integrated" service delivery entity to better help clients and gain greater influence. For example, combine child care and adult care services; combine legal aid, financial counseling, and family counseling services.

10. Establish national goals and standards for nonprofits to increase sector quality, public awareness, and public support.

11. Form a consortium with other nonprofits who serve similar constituents to take advantage of block grants resulting from federal devolution.

12. Facilitate networks and collaboration by making your space available for such activities.

13. Find ways to work with local providers of educational services at all levels.

---

[20] *Readers interested in learning more about collaboration may find help in the Wilder Publishing Center's paired publications,* Collaboration: What Makes It Work *and* Collaboration Handbook: Creating, Sustaining, and Enjoying the Journey. *(See the order form at the back of this book.)*

Engage the community

1. Seek funding to help those constituents least able to represent themselves have a voice. For example, a family-serving program sought funds to provide child care and work stipends so working poor could be involved in key meetings that would affect service delivery.

2. Involve parents, religious organizations, civic groups, and schools in teaching children the value of community involvement and philanthropy.

3. Connect with local media to inform the community about issues related to your mission. For example, in St. Paul, Minnesota, the Wilder Foundation has worked closely with the *St. Paul Pioneer Press* to identify and bring public attention to social services issues that face St. Paul's urban core.

4. Show the community that your crisis is everyone's crisis. For example, a struggling street performance group convened a meeting of local community and business leaders to discuss the positive impact of public arts as well as the fiscal crisis it faced. The meeting focused on the organization's mission and its outcomes, *not* on how to save the organization.

5. Hold mealtime forums (breakfast or lunch is typical) to discuss community issues and to showcase how the community, through its nonprofits and their partners, is resolving those issues.

6. Organize issues groups with community religious congregations, small businesses, neighborhood clubs, schools, and so forth to discuss community goals.

Engage the business community

1. Form partnerships with the business community; find a corporate host that will provide space, staff, funds, resources, or technical assistance.

2. Advocate for your values and goals even as you ask for the involvement and assistance of the business community.

3. Know the people, values, and goals of the businesses you are engaging.

4. Show businesses how they and their community will benefit from your organization's vision for the future. Explain the different roles each sector plays in that vision and focus on the role they might play.

5. Link with businesses that will benefit from the positive public relations your cause will generate.

6. Network with small and midsize businesses who may have more of a stake in (and understanding of) the local community. Seek out those with a leadership role in the community or with potential for growth.

7. Show businesses how to move beyond financial support to become involved in community issues that affect them, their productivity, their employees, or their customers. Engage them through in-kind contributions, use of space or other resources, employee volunteers, and so forth.

8. Collaborate with businesses and other nonprofits to create "incubators" where new, innovative organizations can work to solve problems of the community, sharing space, equipment, and so forth. Use this innovative approach to attract funders and increase corporate interest.

9. Form nonprofit/for-profit partnerships to advocate for common interests. For example, in response to the government's declining role in providing affordable housing, nonprofits have joined with businesses, through the Low Income Housing Tax Credit, to increase the availability of affordable housing.

10. Form partnerships with businesses to train and retrain the workforce as it relates to your current mission.

Engage the public/government sector

1. Advocate for tax incentives that encourage businesses to be involved in community efforts.

2. Use the public schools to teach philanthropy, and set up student-operated philanthropies at schools and universities.

3. Seek ways to work with educational institutions at all grade levels, public and private, nonprofit and for-profit. Schools, colleges, and universities are a rich source of volunteers, technical advice, connections with other resources and institutions, and opportunities for partnership.

4. Advocate for a nonprofit contribution checkoff on tax forms.

5. Make charitable giving a tax credit rather than a deduction, so that those people who don't itemize deductions will have an incentive to donate.

6. Use publicly owned facilities as a site for delivering nonprofit community services.

Postscript

The traditional distinctions between the sectors of our community are beginning to soften. Nonprofit organizations, by using strategies of engagement to reach more people in more ways, will blur the boundaries between nonprofit, government, business, and other sectors of society. We think this will help to increase a sense of community that many people feel is missing today.

The distinctions that separated nonprofits from business, from government, and from other sectors of our society may not serve us well in the future. Successful board members, nonprofit leaders, and their organizations will need to focus outward, on the communities they serve, using their energy to connect with other groups, yet concentrating all the while on the nonprofit's mission in the community.

The traditional ways of operating a nonprofit will be augmented by important connections deep into the community in which the nonprofit works. Nonprofits will assume new roles as conveners, engagers, and partners in helping communities achieve their visions.

As a nonprofit leader, you will need to be flexible, adapting yourself and your organization to the change in how our society wants to meet community needs. You are uniquely positioned to help make the changes discussed in this book. We hope you gained ideas to help your organization manage the challenges ahead.

"Something there is that doesn't love a wall, That wants it torn down."

Robert Frost

APPENDIX A
Strategies Checklist

This checklist of strategies is adapted from our larger list in Chapter 4.
We reduced the list to a more general one in the hopes that you could use it
as a brainstorming tool and checklist for strategies you are already using or
may enact.

Financial Strategies A: Cut or Control Costs

Analyze purchasing
- ☐ Improve purchasing procedures
- ☐ Seek in-kind contributions
- ☐ Network to get better prices on supplies
- ☐ Seek new competitive bids and new suppliers
- ☐ Analyze purchases to see if they are necessary
- ☐ Simplify paperwork and forms; use electronic files
- ☐ Refurbish and reuse supplies

Adjust payables
- ☐ Consolidate or restructure debt
- ☐ Negotiate delayed or reduced payments
- ☐ Barter for needed services

Evaluate facilities and infrastructure
- ☐ Share space or maintenance costs
- ☐ Delay maintenance
- ☐ Save space by moving, reducing size, using home offices, or using split shifts
- ☐ Negotiate a decreased rent with your landlord
- ☐ Find a cheaper phone system; eliminate toll-free lines
- ☐ Eliminate or consolidate newsletters and brochures
- ☐ Eliminate vehicles or shift to less costly vehicles
- ☐ Save energy

Modify staffing and related costs
- ☐ Reduce hours or workweek
- ☐ Cut, freeze, or delay wages;
- ☐ Lay off staff; offer voluntary separation; offer unpaid leave; remove poor performers
- ☐ Freeze hiring
- ☐ Share jobs, consolidate staff, increase workload
- ☐ Use volunteers and graduate interns
- ☐ Hire temporary staff or consultants
- ☐ Remove management layers; don't funnel high performers into management merely to reward them
- ☐ Reduce benefits, staff training, and staff development
- ☐ Limit or eliminate travel
- ☐ Cancel subscriptions; use the Internet and libraries
- ☐ Cancel professional association memberships
- ☐ Switch to a direct reimbursement status for unemployment compensation
- ☐ Ask board not to submit expenses for reimbursement
- ☐ Convert some paid staff to volunteers
- ☐ Share staff with other organizations

Reduce services

- ☐ Analyze your programs and services against your mission and financial goals
- ☐ Reduce or eliminate noncore programs
- ☐ Limit eligibility for programs; reduce the number of clients served
- ☐ Reduce or eliminate core programs
- ☐ Temporarily shut down some or all services
- ☐ Plan to go out of business humanely

Financial Strategies B: Increase Revenues

Manage money differently

- ☐ Speed the inflow of cash by invoicing promptly or offering incentives
- ☐ Try to get grants in the door earlier than the promised date
- ☐ Change management of cash reserves to improve unearned income
- ☐ Sell assets
- ☐ Spend down reserves
- ☐ Borrow money
- ☐ Diversify your sources of income

Increase fees

- ☐ Analyze all the costs of providing a service
- ☐ Change fee structure to result in increased income

Initiate or accelerate fund-raising

- ☐ Research the larger community and current donors to improve response
- ☐ Hire development director or staff
- ☐ Add special events, fund drives, charitable gambling
- ☐ Increase board involvement in fund-raising
- ☐ Increase planned giving
- ☐ Build an endowment
- ☐ Find new donors and diversify funding base
- ☐ Reach out to under-asked populations
- ☐ Collaborate on fund drives; join a federated fund drive
- ☐ Mobilize everyone in the search for new resources
- ☐ Link with a business or credit card company to receive a percentage of sales
- ☐ Seek in-kind contributions that can be converted to cash
- ☐ Increase the search for foundation and government grants

Expand or add services

- ☐ Boost enrollment in or expand offerings of successful services
- ☐ Sell staff expertise and time
- ☐ Add income-generating product or service that fufills mission
- ☐ Rent office space or equipment to others
- ☐ Sell valuable information that others need
- ☐ Seek related niche markets
- ☐ Charge others for a service you also use (for example, maintenance)
- ☐ Develop a catalog of products used by your organization and other nonprofits
- ☐ Charge a fee to serve as the fiscal agent for other organizations

Increase productivity

- ☐ Provide incentives for productive staff
- ☐ Simplify production or service without loss of quality
- ☐ Invest in an educated staff; provide training as needed
- ☐ Research and implement "best practice" in all functions
- ☐ Upgrade staff while cutting back
- ☐ Invest in technology that improves productivity

Structural Strategies

Modify the mission

- ☐ Reexamine the mission and realign the organization accordingly
- ☐ Modify the mission to build clients' capacity to solve their own problems
- ☐ Change the mission to enable the organization to respond to rapidly changing conditions
- ☐ Move out of direct support services and into prevention services
- ☐ Be a pilot site for some foundation, academic, or government program

Modify the organization's structure

- ☐ Eliminate programs that are redundant with those of other organizations or combine them to improve services
- ☐ Position yourself higher in the "food chain" when intense competition accompanies a changing environment
- ☐ Respond to a changing environment by changing programs
- ☐ Spin off a struggling or "orphan" program to another organization where it has a better chance to thrive

☐ Merge with or acquire a competitor's or an ally's program

☐ Relocate with a group of related organizations to form a one-stop shop

☐ Become a for-profit; add a for-profit subsidiary; be acquired by a for-profit

Modify the organization's culture

☐ Enlist the support of potential funders as you modify your programs, and then request funds to support changes

☐ Share resources and expenses with other organizations that have similar needs

☐ Make your services more culturally sensitive

☐ Educate the board of directors to make them more effective

☐ Mobilize everyone in the organization to help market its mission, message, services, and needs

☐ Tear down bureaucracies that interfere with the creative flow of ideas

☐ Replicate rather than reinvent

☐ Link with a complementary but different organization to bring resources into the organization

☐ Take a more entrepreneurial approach to accomplishing your mission

Engagement Strategies

Engage other nonprofits

☐ Work with state and national nonprofit associations

☐ Form associations to negotiate with contracting agencies as a block

☐ Establish cooperative programs with other nonprofits to increase the number of stakeholders in each other's organization

☐ Collaborate with like-minded nonprofits; seek funding to support collaboration

☐ Develop a bartering resource system among nonprofits

☐ Create a nonprofit organization to insure nonprofits; return surplus income to policyholders

☐ Pool funds with other nonprofits to get a better return on the investment of capital

☐ Acquire or merge with another nonprofit whose services complement yours

☐ Establish national goals and standards for nonprofits to increase sector quality, public awareness, and public support

☐ Form a consortium with other nonprofits to take advantage of federal block grants

☐ Facilitate networks and collaboration by making your space available for such activities

☐ Find ways to work with local providers of educational services at all levels

Engage the community

☐ Seek funding to help those constituents least able to represent themselves have a voice

☐ Involve all members of the community in teaching children the value of community involvement and philanthropy

☐ Connect with local media to inform the community about issues related to your mission

☐ Show the community that your crisis is a community crisis

☐ Hold community issues forums; discuss community goals

Engage the business community

☐ Form partnerships with businesses; find a host that will provide space, staff, funds, resources, or technical assistance

☐ Advocate for your organization's values and goals while seeking business involvement

☐ Know the people, values, and goals of the businesses you are engaging

☐ Share your vision of the future with businesses so they can see how they and their community will benefit

☐ Link with businesses that will benefit from the positive public relations your organization's cause will generate

☐ Network with small and midsize businesses with a personal stake in the local community

☐ Show businesses how to get involved in community issues that affect them

☐ Collaborate with businesses and other nonprofits to create "incubators" for new, innovative organizations

☐ Form nonprofit/for-profit partnerships to advocate for common interests

Engage the public/government sector

☐ Advocate for tax incentives that encourage businesses to be involved in community efforts

☐ Use the public schools to teach philanthropy; set up student-operated philanthropies at schools and universities

☐ Seek ways to work with educational institutions at all grade levels, public and private, nonprofit and for-profit.

☐ Advocate for a nonprofit contribution checkoff on tax forms

☐ Advocate for making charitable giving a tax credit rather than a deduction

☐ Use publicly owned facilities as a site for delivering nonprofit community services

APPENDIX B
Reproducible Worksheets

This worksheet will help you understand where you are going as an organization. It should be a quick reference based on your strategic plan. (If you do not have a current strategic plan, you will need to go through a process that at least addresses the following four areas: values, mission, core competencies, and vision.)

Write a brief paragraph that summarizes your position for each of these four points.

1. What are your organization's philosophy and core values? (Beliefs central to your organization; what your organization holds most important.)

2. What is your organization's mission? (Your organization's purpose; what it intends to accomplish; the reason it exists.)

3. What are your organization's two to four core competencies? (Its greatest strengths; what it does best; how it adds value to the community.)

4. What is your organization's vision? (How the world will be different because your organization exists; what role your organization will play in making that difference.)

This worksheet will help you clarify how you make decisions as an organization. It will also help you decide if you want to change how you make decisions and who makes them.

Write a brief paragraph that summarizes your position for these two questions.

1. How have you approached decision making in similar situations in the past? Who made decisions and how were they made? Typically, who makes decisions and how are they made?

(continued)

2. Given what you've read in Chapter 2, do you want to approach decision making differently in the future? If so, what do you want to change? Who will make decisions and how will they be made?

This worksheet will help you clarify the nature, cause, and size of the problem or opportunity facing your organization.

Write a brief paragraph in response to each of the following questions.

1. What is the community problem or opportunity? (For example, a 50 percent increase in the homeless population; an opportunity to create a neighborhood arts center.)

2. What is the cause of the problem or opportunity? (For example, elimination of a government program; emergence of a grassroots group with interests in culture and education.)

(continued)

3. What is the size of this problem or opportunity? (In terms of people, dollars, numbers of cultural programs per capita—whatever measurement seems to fit the problem.)

4. Now combine your answers to questions 1, 2, and 3 into a problem or opportunity statement. Whenever possible frame statements positively, recognizing the opportunities in any given situation.

This worksheet will help you understand the scope and magnitude of the financial reductions facing your organization.

1. Construct a conservative budget based on the revenue cuts your organization faces.

    a. What revenues are definite or very probable? Include revenues when you know the funding has been approved. (Attach a dollar figure.)
    b. Are the funds restricted for specific programs, or are they for general support? (State which programs receive restricted funding.)
    c. What are the implications of any funding cuts for other funders or fee-based income? For example, if a major funder pulls out, sapping 80 percent of a program's budget, will other contributors withdraw their support? (Attach a dollar figure to the reduction; be sure to decrease the revenue assumptions by this amount.)
    d. Given these figures, construct a conservative program budget. Include only those funds of which you are certain. Once you have identified revenues, complete the budget by entering expenses. Use the chart in Worksheet 2B to enter revenues and expenses. (WARNING: Assume no new revenue sources. To do so is to set yourself up for failure. You must plan from a conservative budget.)

Conservative Budget						
			Specify Each Program/Service			
Revenues	Total	Admin.				
TOTAL REVENUE						
Personnel Operating Expenses						
Salaries						
Payroll Taxes						
Employee Benefits						
TOTAL PERSONNEL						

(continued)

Revenues	Total	Admin.	Specify Each Program/Service			
Conservative Budget (continued)						
Other Operating Expenses						
Business Expense						
Program						
Office						
Development						
Fund-raising						
TOTAL OTHER EXPENSES						
TOTAL EXPENSES						

2. Which programs (services) are in jeopardy?

   a. Which programs cannot be operated unless there is more funding?

   b. Which programs will need to be significantly cut or will require restructuring to continue?

   c. Which programs depend on new sources of funding that are less certain, such as client fees for service, third-party reimbursement, or individual donors?

3. Now state your problem in terms of

   a. The program that will be affected

   b. The dollars that will be lost

   c. The impact on the organization and staff

   d. The impact on clients/customers

   e. The impact on the community

This worksheet will help you identify individuals and groups to involve in developing criteria, generating strategies, and selecting the best strategies. As you choose people to involve and decide how to involve them, you will also be making choices about the degree to which you want to involve various sectors of the community.

Chapter 2 described four arenas of influence. These were:

Take Care of Business—Operate with those people who are part of the organization (the board, staff, key volunteers)

Bet on the Board (and Its Network)—Broaden your involvement to include board members' contacts in the community, with business groups, and with other organizations

Work with Your Allies and Partners—Involve organizations with whom you share history, common interests, values, missions, constituents, and so forth

Come to the Table—Engage the community in the broadest possible way

Give some thought to the arenas above, and then choose who to involve. You might select people because of what or who they know, because they have a stake in the same problem or opportunity that your organization faces, or because their support is critical. As you identify individuals and groups, write them on the chart below. Also decide how you want to involve them (part or all of Steps 4, 5, and 6) and place a check mark for the steps in which you'll involve them.

Participants	Step 4 (Criteria)	Step 5 (Brainstorm)	Step 6 (Selection)
Board members			
Staff leaders			
Other staff			

(continued)

Participants	Step 4 (Criteria)	Step 5 (Brainstorm)	Step 6 (Selection)
Key volunteers			
Board members' and volunteers' networks			
Allies/partners			
Clients/customers and their representatives			
Collaborators			

Participants	Step 4 (Criteria)	Step 5 (Brainstorm)	Step 6 (Selection)
Funders			
Contracting organizations			
Referral sources and referents			
Competitors			
Government agencies, regulators, officials			
Local businesses and corporations			

(continued)

Participants	Step 4 (Criteria)	Step 5 (Brainstorm)	Step 6 (Selection)
Religious organizations			
Funders you have not worked with			
Community and civic groups			
Media			
Others			

This worksheet will help you develop the work plan you will undertake in order to accomplish Steps 4 (Criteria), 5 (Brainstorm), and 6 (Selection).

List below the tasks necessary to carry out Steps 4, 5, and 6. For each task decide who is responsible and specify a deadline. Remember to carefully consider *who* will invite each person to participate. The sample work plan on page 43 may help you think about the level of detail you need.

Task	Responsible	By When

This worksheet will help you develop and select three to five criteria for choosing the best strategies to deal with the problems or opportunities facing your organization. Criteria should express the organization's values and mission.

Use questions 1–4 below to help you generate criteria, or use some other process you are familiar with. Use question 5 to write out three to five criteria for success. Also enter these on Worksheet 6: Select the Viable Strategies.

1. What specific conditions related to your values, mission, and vision must be part of any solution? (For example: *Any solution must maintain our position as the leading advocate for people with developmental disabilities. Or . . . Any solution must enable us to continue to expand into the neighboring county. Or . . . We must maintain all services that provide support to victims.*)

2. Are there conditions that must be met regarding customers or clients? (For example: *Any solution must keep our homeless shelter open for one hundred people because we have a commitment to the city. Or . . . Any solution must keep services free to our clients.*)

(continued)

3. Are there financial conditions that need to be solved in any solution, such as cash flow, diversification, restrictions to funding, or timing? (For example: *Any solution must have us operating with a balanced budget within six months. Or . . . Any solution needs to honor the fact that the Bush Foundation grant is restricted to providing jobs for homeless people.*)

4. What other factors should be part of judging any solutions, such as staffing, services, public perception, time frame, or special relationships with funders? (For example: *Any solution needs to keep our most visible storefront clinics open. Or . . . Any solution will not affect services that we provide in support of the city's public health department.*)

5. Select the three to five most important criteria that you will use in determining the best strategies for addressing the opportunity or problem.

This worksheet will help the strategy-generating group develop options. Question 1 and question 2 should be filled out by the nonprofit leader.

1. Write your problem or opportunity statement here. (This is from Worksheets 2A or 2B. To be completed by the nonprofit leader.)

2. *Optional:* Write your desired outcome here. (To be completed by the nonprofit leader.)

(continued)

3. Generate strategies that will achieve the desired outcome or address the problem or opportunity as stated. Strategies may be stated as direct solutions or as processes that will lead to as yet undetermined solutions. Brainstorm as many strategies as you can. Then pick the very best ones and flesh out the details, suggesting steps, who might be involved, and helpful resources.

Strategy:

Strategy:

Strategy:

Strategy:

Strategy:

Strategy:

This worksheet will help you decide which strategies to implement by comparing them with the criteria established in Step 4.

List strategies down the first column. List criteria in shorthand at the top of each of the next columns. Then determine which strategies best meet the criteria by ranking them on a scale of 1–3 (3 being the best fit). The strategies with the highest total are the best candidates for implementation. Circle the strategy or strategies you will use.

Strategy	Criteria					Total Rank
	1. _____ _____	2. _____ _____	3. _____ _____	4. _____ _____	5. _____ _____	
A.						
B.						
C.						
D.						
E.						
F.						

This worksheet will help you develop an implementation plan for each strategy.

State the strategy, and then list the tasks required to implement that strategy. Identify who is responsible for each task and by when the task should be accomplished.

Strategy/Tasks	Responsible	By When

APPENDIX C
Survey Responses

I n the course of our research for this book, we conducted a survey of nonprofit organizations. We used a series of open-ended questions. After collecting responses, we placed them into categories. From these categories we developed the taxonomy of cutback responses that you read in Chapter 4, although that listing includes many more strategies than our survey respondents supplied.

Our survey was a fishing expedition, not a scientific poll, and please keep that in mind as you read the tables. After several interviews with nonprofit leaders, we drafted questions to help nonprofits focus on the area of cutbacks. With the help of the Wilder Foundation Research Center, we turned those questions into the survey. During summer 1996 we distributed two hundred surveys via the mail and also made the survey available on the online nonprofit information and communication service, HandsNet.

Sixty-five organizations responded to the survey; but, since two of them did not respond to the survey questions, the data represents sixty-three organizations. Here's an overview of what they told us, followed by tables showing the numbers of responses.

- The types of organizations responding included human services (54 percent); health, mental health, and medical research (14 percent); education related (13 percent); and arts, culture, and humanities (6 percent).

- Organizations responding ranged in size from those with an annual budget of less than $100,000 to those with an annual budget greater than $10 million. Most were in the ranges of $100,000 to $500,000 (37 percent); $500,000 to $1 million (24 percent); or $1 million to $5 million (22 percent).

- Seventy-six percent of the respondents said they anticipated a cut in funding for one or more of their services.

- Cuts were anticipated across the board, including federal funding (50 percent); state funding (46 percent); local government funding (31 percent); and philanthropic funding (38 percent).

- Of the many strategies planned for coping with cutbacks, the most frequently cited were to implement fund-raising (75 percent); modify staffing and its costs (53 percent); control operating costs (30 percent); and reduce services (19 percent).

The tables that follow provide greater detail about these responses.

Table 1: Do You Anticipate a Reduction in Funding?

	Number
Yes	48
No	15
Total	**63**

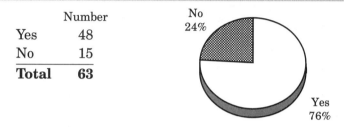

Table 2: Anticipated Loss of Funding

	N = 48
1. Federal funding	24
2. State funding	22
3. Philanthropic or foundation funding	18
4. Local government funding	15
5. No funding source indicated	3

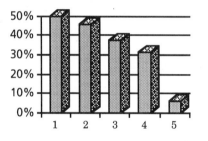

Table 3: Organization's Annual Budget

	N = 63
1. Less than $100,000	2
2. $100,000 - $500,000	23
3. $500,000 - $1 million	15
4. $1 million - $5 million	14
5. $5 million - $10 million	2
6. Greater than $10 million	5
7. Data missing	2

Table 4: Type of Nonprofit Organization

	N = 63
1. Human services	34
2. Health, mental health, medical research	9
3. Education related	8
4. Arts, culture, humanities	4
5. Environment/animal related	3
6. Management consulting	2
7. Other	2
8. Religion related	1

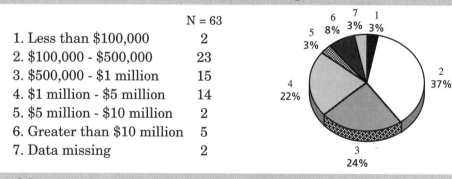

Table 5: Strategy Use by Major Category

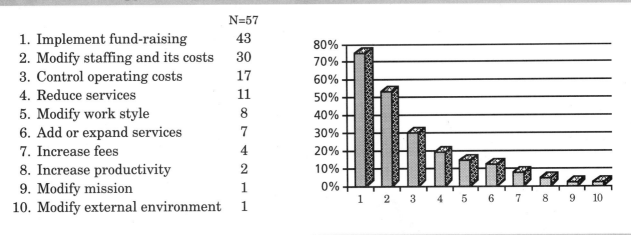

		N=57
1.	Implement fund-raising	43
2.	Modify staffing and its costs	30
3.	Control operating costs	17
4.	Reduce services	11
5.	Modify work style	8
6.	Add or expand services	7
7.	Increase fees	4
8.	Increase productivity	2
9.	Modify mission	1
10.	Modify external environment	1

Table 6: Control Operating Costs

Number of organizations that will or would control operating costs

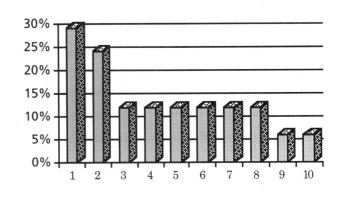

		N=17
1.	Seek in-kind contributions	5
2.	Delay payments	4
3.	General cost cutting (nonspecific response)	2
4.	Control supplies	2
5.	Decrease benefits	2
6.	Delay purchases	2
7.	Improve purchasing	2
8.	Identify and cut ineffective/ unnecessary practices	2
9.	Share space	1
10.	Delay maintenance	1

Table 7: Modify Staffing and Its Costs

Number of organizations that will or would modify staffing and its costs

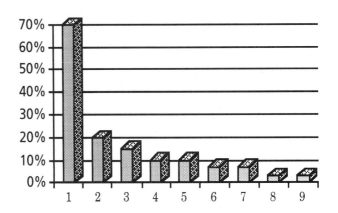

		N=30
1.	Lay off staff	21
2.	Increase workload	6
3.	Use volunteers	4
4.	Share jobs or consolidate staff	3
5.	Cut or freeze wages	3
6.	Reduce hours	2
7.	Freeze/delay hiring	2
8.	Hire temporary staff/ consultants ("outsource")	1
9.	Offer unpaid leaves of absence	1

Table 8: Reduce Services

Number of organizations that will or would reduce services

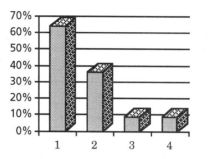

	N=11
1. Reduce or eliminate core program or service	7
2. General reduction of services (nonspecific response)	4
3. Reduce or eliminate noncore program or service	1
4. Limit eligibility	1

Table 9: Increase/Implement Fund-raising

Number of organizations that will or would increase fund-raising

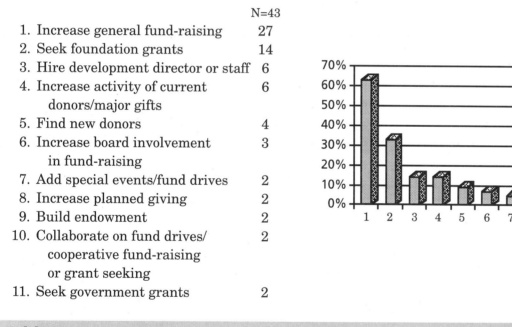

	N=43
1. Increase general fund-raising	27
2. Seek foundation grants	14
3. Hire development director or staff	6
4. Increase activity of current donors/major gifts	6
5. Find new donors	4
6. Increase board involvement in fund-raising	3
7. Add special events/fund drives	2
8. Increase planned giving	2
9. Build endowment	2
10. Collaborate on fund drives/ cooperative fund-raising or grant seeking	2
11. Seek government grants	2

Table 10: Increase Fees

Number of organizations that will or would increase fees = 4

Table 11: Add or Expand Services

Number of organizations that will or would expand services

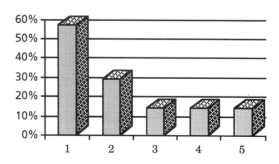

	N=7
1. General add or expand (nonspecific response)	4
2. Add earned-income generating service	2
3. Sell staff time to other organizations	1
4. Rent office space or equipment to others	1
5. Beef up core services	1

Table 12: Increase Productivity

Number of organizations that will or would increase productivity

	N=2
Increase productivity. General (nonspecific response)	1
Incentives for income-producing staff	1
Change mix of productive/support staff	1

Table 13: Modify Mission

Number of organizations that will or would modify mission = 1

Table 14: Modify Work Style

Number of organizations that will or would modify work style

	N=8
1. Collaborate with other nonprofits	3
2. Partner with business community	3
3. Restructure service delivery	3
4. Add a for-profit subsidiary	2
5. Acquire or merge with another nonprofit	1
6. Be acquired by a for-profit	1
7. Be more entrepreneurial	1
8. Become a pilot site	1

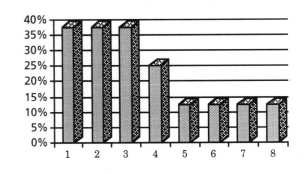

Table 15: Modify External Environment

Number of organizations that will or would modify the external environment

Modify social environment	1
Modify legislative/regulatory environment	1

Bibliography

Following is a selected list of the documents we reviewed while developing this book. We placed icons by more recent documents that may help you grapple with the challenges and opportunities presented by the changing relationship between the federal government and nonprofit organizations. Publications marked with this symbol 📖 help in understanding devolution. Publications marked with this symbol 🖋 help in developing financial, structural, or engagement strategies or in coping with the impact of change on an organization.

📖 Abramson, Alan J., and Lester M. Salamon. "The Nonprofit Sector and the Federal Budget: FY 1998 Congressional Budget Resolution." Document prepared for Independent Sector. June 27, 1997. Independent Sector Web site (http://indepsec.org/cngrtxt.html).

Adzies, Ichak. "Organizational Passages: Diagnosing and Treating Lifecycle Problems of Organizations." *Organizational Dynamics* 8 (Summer 1979): 2-25.

AFSCME Public Policy Department. "Safety Net for Sale . . . Why Social Welfare Program Administration Should Not Be Privatized." 1996. Document in the Substantive Law Forum of HandsNet Web site (http://www.handsnet.org).

Amherst H. Wilder Foundation Cutback Management Seminars file notes, 1984-1989.

Bane, Mary Jo. "Welfare as We Might Know It." *The American Prospect* 30 (January-February 1997): 47-53. Document on Electronic Policy Network Web site (http://epn.org/prospect/30/30bane.html).

🖋 Barry, Bryan W. *Strategic Planning Workbook for Nonprofit Organizations, Revised and Updated.* St. Paul, Minn.: Amherst H. Wilder Foundation, 1997.

Behn, Robert D. "Cutback Budgeting." *Journal of Policy Analysis and Management* 4 (1985): 155-77.

Bernstein, Jeremy. "Profiles: Allocating Sacrifice." *The New Yorker* 59 (January 28, 1983): 45-78.

Bridges, William. *Surviving Corporate Transitions: Rational Management in a World of Mergers, Layoffs, Start-ups, Divestitures, Deregulation, and New Technologies.* New York: Doubleday, 1988.

Bridges, William. *Managing Transitions: Making the Most of Change.* Reading, Mass.: Addison-Wesley, 1991.

Brinckerhoff, Peter C. *Mission-Based Management: Leading Your Not-for-Profit into the 21st Century.* Dillon, Colo.: Alpine Guild, 1994.

Brinckerhoff, Peter C. "What the Next Years Will Bring and How to Get Ready." *Nonprofit World* 13 (March-April 1995): 19-22.

Brinckerhoff, Peter C. *Financial Empowerment: More Money for More Mission.* Dillon, Colo.: Alpine Guild, 1996.

Brinckerhoff, Peter C. "How to Save Money Through Bottoms-Up Budgeting." *Nonprofit World* 14 (January-February 1996): 22-24.

Brinkley, Alan. "The Assault on Government." (Date unknown). Document on Electronic Policy Institute Web site (http://epn.org/tcf/brinkley.html).

Brockner, Joel, Jeff Greenberg, Audrey Brockner, Jenny Bortz, Jeanette Davy, and Carolyn Carter. "Layoffs, Equity Theory, and Work Performance: Further Evidence of the Impact of Survivor Guilt." *Academy of Management Journal* 29 (1986): 373-84.

Broussard, William J. "The Dynamics of the Group Outplacement Workshop." *Personnel Journal* (December 1979).

"Budget Cuts: Full Effect Yet to Be Felt." April 4, 1996. Document on HandsNet Web site (http://www.handsnet.org).

Burlingame, Dwight F., William A. Diaz, and Warren F. Ilchman. *Capacity for Change? The Nonprofit World in the Age of Devolution.* Indianapolis: Indiana University Center on Philanthropy, 1996.

Cameron, Kim, and Raymond Zammutto. "Matching Managerial Strategies to Conditions of Decline." *Human Resource Management* 22 (Winter 1983): 356-75.

Center for Community Change. "How and Why to Influence Public Policy: An Action Guide for Community Organizations." *Community Change* 17 (Winter 1996): 2-39.

Curley, Bob. "Generating Revenue from Unlikely In-Kind Donations." May 17, 1996. Document on HandsNet Web site (http://www.handsnet.org).

Curley, Bob. "Offenders Can Make Donations Rather Than Paying Fines." May 17, 1996. Document on HandsNet Web site (http://www.handsnet.org).

DeLuca, Joel R., Michael Kitson, and Kathleen Morris. "The Downsizing Dilemma: Getting the Cuts, Keeping the Commitment." *OD Practitioner* 17 (September 1985): 1-4.

Denver Children's Museum. *Nonprofit Piggy Goes to Market.* Denver, Colo.: Denver Children's Museum, 1984.

"The Devolution Revolution: Challenge and Opportunity." *NFG Reports: The Newsletter of the Neighborhood Funders Group* 3 (Spring 1996): 11-12.

DiMauro, Bob. "The Role of Organization Development in Reducing Workforce." *OD Practitioner* 17 (September 1985): 10-13.

Eadie, Douglas C. *Beyond Strategic Planning: How to Involve Nonprofit Boards in Growth and Change.* Washington, D.C.: National Center for Nonprofit Boards, 1993.

Egan, Anne Hays. *The Devolution Toolkit: Building Capacity.* Two editions of a work in progress, July 1996; July 1997. Santa Fe, New Mexico.

Etsy, Katherine. "The Dynamics of the Declining Organization and OD Frontier." Paper presented at the OD Network National Conference, Lake Geneva, Wisconsin, September 29-October 6, 1982.

Galaskieicz, Joseph, Sarah Allen, Wolfgang Bielefeld, Tammie Bougies, Naomi Kaufman, Alisa Potter, and Kay Schaffer. *Corporate-Nonprofit Linkages in Minneapolis-St. Paul: Findings from a Longitudinal Study 1980-1988.* Minneapolis: University of Minnesota Department of Sociology, 1990.

Giving Forum. "Grantmaking in the 'Post-Federal' Era." *Giving Forum* 19 (Winter 1996): 1, 4-6.

Goldberg, Lenny. "Come the Devolution." *The American Prospect* 24 (Winter 1995): 66-71 (http://epn.org/prospect/24/24gold.html).

Greenstein, Robert, Richard Kagan, and Marion Nichols. "Bearing Most of the Burden: How Deficit Reduction During the 104th Congress Concentrated on Programs for the Poor." (December 1996). Document on Center on Budget and Policy Priorities Web site (http://www.cbpp.org/104th.htm).

Hall, Holly. "Planning Ahead for Survival." *Chronicle of Philanthropy* 8 (January 11, 1996): 22.

Hatry, Harry, Therese van Houten, Margaret C. Platz, and Martha Taylor Greenway. *Measuring Program Outcomes: A Practical Approach.* Alexandria, Va.: United Way of America, 1996.

Hayes, Cheryl D. with assistance from Anna E. Danneggar. "Rethinking Block Grants: Toward an Improved Intergovernmental Financing for Education and Other Children's Services." Monograph from the Finance Project, Washington, D.C., 1996.

Hirschhorn, Larry, et al. *Cutting Back: Retrenchment and Redevelopment in Human and Community Services.* San Francisco: Jossey-Bass, 1983.

Hodgkinson, Virginia A., Lester M. Salamon, et al. "The Impact of Federal Budget Proposals upon the Activities of Charitable Organizations and the People They Serve, 1996-2002: The 100 Nonprofit Organizations Study." Washington, D.C.: Independent Sector, 1996.

Hopfensperger, Jean. "Report Warns Nonprofits to Brace for Impact." *Minneapolis Star Tribune*, November 7, 1995.

Hosek, James, and Robert Levine, eds. "The New Fiscal Federalism and the Social Safety Net: A View from California." 1996. Document on the Rand organization's Web site (http://www.rand.org/publications/CF/CF123).

Independent Sector Press Release. "New Independent Sector Study Finds Giving and Volunteering Rising." (October 9, 1996). Document on Independent Sector Web site (http://www.indepsec.org/gvrel.html).

"Information About Nonprofit/For-Profit Partnerships." (Date unknown). Document on HandsNet Web site (http://www.handsnet.org).

Kincaid, John. "Foreword: The New Federalism Context of the New Judicial Federalism." (Date unknown). Document on Rutgers University Web site (http://camlaw.rutgers.edu/publications/lawjournal/kincaid.html).

Kingston, Tom. Memo to Chris Park. "Wilder Foundation Response to Devolution." (Date unknown). Amherst H. Wilder Foundation.

Landy, Laura. *Something Ventured, Something Gained: A Business Development Guide for Nonprofit Organizations.* New York: American Council for the Arts, 1989.

Lippitt, Gordon, and Ronald Lippit. "'Downsizing'—How to Manage More with Less." *Management Review* 71 (March 1982): 9-14.

Lippitt, Ronald. "Managing Effectively with Limited Resources." Chap. 3 in *Management Development and Training Handbook,* edited by Bernard Taylor and Gordon Lippit, 2d ed. London: McGraw-Hill, 1983.

Lorange, Peter, and Robert Nelson. "How to Recognize—and Avoid—Organizational Decline." *Sloan Management Review* 28 (Spring 1987): 41-48.

"LSC [Legal Services Corporation] Lawyers Cope with Cuts." September 15, 1996. Document on HandsNet Web site (http://www.handsnet.org).

Lukermann, Barbara, Madeleine Kimmich, and Lester M. Salamon. *The Twin Cities Nonprofit Sector in a Time of Government Retrenchment.* Washington, D.C.: Urban Institute, 1984.

Mattessich, Paul W., and Barbara R. Monsey. *Collaboration: What Makes It Work.* St. Paul, Minn.: Amherst H. Wilder Foundation, 1992.

Mattessich, Paul W., and Barbara R. Monsey. *Community Building: What Makes It Work.* St. Paul, Minn.: Amherst H. Wilder Foundation, 1997.

McCormack, Patrick J. "Nonprofits at the Brink: Lean Budgets, Growing Needs, and the Fate of Nonprofits." (Date unknown). Document on Minnesota Council of Nonprofits Web site (http://www.mncn.org/newfed/brink.htm#cuts).

McDonnell, Lynda. "Nonprofits Prepare for Future Pain: 'Devolution' Their Version of Private Sector Downsizing." *St. Paul Pioneer Press*, May 20, 1996.

McLaughlin, Thomas A. *Seven Steps to a Nonprofit Merger.* Washington, D.C.: National Center for Nonprofit Boards, 1996.

McTighe, John J. "Management Strategies to Deal with Shrinking Resources." *Public Administration Review* 39 (January-February 1979): 86-90.

Miles, Robert H. *The Organizational Life Cycle.* San Francisco: Jossey-Bass, 1980.

Miliken, Frances. "Three Types of Perceived Uncertainty About the Environment: State, Effect, and Response Uncertainty." *Academy of Management Review* 12 (1987): 133-43.

Nadler, David. "Managing Transitions to Uncertain Future States." *Organizational Dynamics* 11 (Summer 1982): 37-45.

National Institute for Literacy. "How to Prepare for Block Grants." October 1995. Document on National Institute for Literacy Web site (http://literacy.nifl.gov/policy/102395.html).

Neugebauer, Roger. "Surviving Tight Times or What to Do When the Money Runs Out." *Exchange* (January 1987): 8-13.

Pettis, Nancy, and John Gray. *Part of the Solution: Innovative Approaches to Nonprofit Funding: Summary Report of the Exploratory Project on Financing the Nonprofit Sector.* Washington, D.C.: Institute for Public Policy and Administration Union for Experimenting Colleges and Universities, October 1988.

Salamon, Lester M. *Holding the Center: America's Nonprofit Sector at a Crossroads.* New York: Nathan Cummings Foundation, 1997.

Salamon, Lester M., and Alan J. Abramson. *The Federal Budget and the Nonprofit Sector.* Washington, D.C.: Urban Institute, 1982.

Salamon, Lester M., David M. Altschuler, and Carol J. DeVita. *Twin Cities Nonprofit Organizations: The Challenge of Retrenchment.* Washington, D.C.: Urban Institute, 1984-1985.

Seltzer, Michael. *Securing Your Organization's Future: A Complete Guide to Fundraising Strategies.* New York: Foundation Center, 1987.

Skloot, Edward, ed. *The Nonprofit Entrepreneur: Creating Ventures to Earn Income.* New York: Foundation Center, 1988.

Soros, George. "The Capitalist Threat," *The Atlantic Monthly* 279 (February 1997): 45-58.

"State Safety Nets Frayed by Welfare Reform." September 22, 1996. Document on HandsNet Web site (http://www.handsnet.org).

Stern, Gary J. *Marketing Workbook for Nonprofit Organizations.* St. Paul, Minn.: Amherst H. Wilder Foundation, 1990.

Stern, Gary J. *Marketing Workbook for Nonprofit Organizations Volume II: Mobilize People for Marketing Success.* St. Paul, Minn.: Amherst H. Wilder Foundation, 1997.

Sturgeon, M. Sue, and Linda J. Shinn. "The Downsizing Dilemma." *Association Management* 39 (August 1987): 91-94.

Sullivan, Kathleen M. "Are the Federalist Papers Still Relevant?" (Date unknown). Document on Electronic Policy Network Web site (http://epn.org/tcf/sullivan.html).

Tomasko, Robert M. *Downsizing: Reshaping the Corporation for the Future.* New York: AMACOM, 1987.

Ukeles, Jacob B. *Doing More with Less: Turning Public Management Around.* New York: AMACOM, 1982.

Wheatley, Margaret. *Leadership and the New Science: Learning About Organization from an Orderly Universe.* San Francisco: Berrett-Koehler, 1994.

Winer, Michael, and Karen Ray. *Collaboration Handbook: Creating, Sustaining, and Enjoying the Journey.* St. Paul, Minn.: Amherst H. Wilder Foundation, 1994.

Young, Dennis R. "Accountability: The Key to Keeping the Nonprofit Sector on Course." August 1996. Document on Charity Village Web site (http://www.charityvillage.com).

Some Helpful Web Sites

There are hundreds of Web sites useful to nonprofits. Any one of the following can link you to other sites or help you research devolution and its impact:

Center on Budget and Policy Priorities	www.cbpp.org
Charity Village	www.charityvillage.com
Electronic Policy Network	www.epn.org
HandsNet	www.handsnet.org
Independent Sector	www.indepsec.org
Indiana University Center on Philanthropy	www.tcop.org
Minnesota Council of Nonprofits	www.mncn.org
Support Center for Nonprofit Management	www.igc.apc.org/sf

Also, we invite you to visit us at the Wilder Foundation Web site. We have placed a list of cutback strategies on that site and will update the strategies quarterly for the first twelve months after the publication of this book. If the experiment is successful and helpful, we will continue to post new strategies as people send them to us.

Our Web site is **www.wilder.org**. Once you reach that site, select the publications menu to find the strategies list.

Notes

Notes

Notes